TIME
Living Wonders
The marvels and mysteries of life on Earth

Fast forward *A cheetah cub eyes the camera; youngsters of the feline species* Acinonyx jubatus *remain close to their mothers until they are 13 to 20 months old and grow up to become the speediest land animals on the planet*

TIME

MANAGING EDITOR Richard Stengel
DEPUTY MANAGING EDITOR Adi Ignatius
ART DIRECTOR Arthur Hochstein

Living Wonders

EDITOR Kelly Knauer
DESIGNER Ellen Fanning
PICTURE EDITOR Patricia Cadley
WRITER Matthew McCann Fenton
RESEARCH Matt Wagner
COPY EDITOR Bruce Christopher Carr

TIME INC. HOME ENTERTAINMENT
PUBLISHER Richard Fraiman
GENERAL MANAGER Steven Sandonato
EXECUTIVE DIRECTOR, MARKETING SERVICES Carol Pittard
DIRECTOR, RETAIL & SPECIAL SALES Tom Mifsud
DIRECTOR, NEW PRODUCT DEVELOPMENT Peter Harper
ASSISTANT DIRECTOR, BRAND MARKETING Joy Butts
ASSOCIATE COUNSEL Helen Wan
SENIOR BRAND MANAGER, TWRS/M Holly Oakes
BOOK PRODUCTION MANAGER Suzanne Janso
DESIGN AND PREPRESS MANAGER Anne-Michelle Gallero
BRAND MANAGER Shelley Rescober

SPECIAL THANKS
Alexandra Bliss, Glenn Buonocore, Susan Chodakiewicz, Margaret Hess, Robert Marasco, Dennis Marcel, Brooke Reger, Mary Sarro-Waite, Ilene Schreider, Adriana Tierno, Alex Voznesenskiy

Copyright 2008 Time Inc. Home Entertainment
Published by TIME Books, Time Inc. • 1271 Avenue of the Americas
New York, NY 10020

All rights reserved. No part of this book may be reproduced in any form or by any electronic or mechanical means, including information storage and retrieval systems, without permission in writing from the publisher, except by a reviewer, who may quote brief passages in a review. TIME and the Red Border Design are protected through trademark registration in the United States and in the foreign countries where TIME magazine circulates. TIME Books is a trademark of Time Inc.

We welcome your comments and suggestions about TIME Books. Please write to us at: TIME Books • Attention: Book Editors • PO Box 11016 • Des Moines, IA 50336-1016

If you would like to order any of our hardcover Collector's Edition books, please call us at 1-800-327-6388 (Monday through Friday, 7 a.m.–8 p.m., or Saturday, 7 a.m.–6 p.m., Central time).

PRINTED IN THE UNITED STATES OF AMERICA

Photography credits

Front cover: Main image, boabab tree, Africa: Jim Zuckerman—Corbis; insets, left to right: diagonal-banded sweetlips, Great Barrier Reef, Australia: Fred Bavendam—Minden Pictures; jaguar, Belize: Gerry Ellis—Minden Pictures; orchid, Borneo: Frans Lanting—Minden Pictures

Back cover, top to bottom: musk oxen, Canada: Jim Brandenburg—Minden Pictures; chimipanzee mother/child, Africa: Anup Shah—Minden Pictures; courting mute swans, the Netherlands: Flip De Nooyer—Minden Pictures; grizzly bear, salmon, Alaska: Matthias Breiter—Minden Pictures

Charge! *Blue wildebeests (Connochaetes taurinus) vault into the Mara River during migration season in the Masai Mara National Reserve, Kenya*

SUZI ESZTERHAS—MINDEN PICTURES

Contents

1
adaptation

rain-forest birds • 4
rain-forest plants • 6
amphibians • 8
reptiles • 10
desert plants • 12
desert animals • 14
grassland animals • 16, 18
shorebirds • 20
snakes • 22
coral reefs • 24
crustaceans • 26
sea creatures • 28, 30
deep-sea fish • 32
squid • 34
penguins • 36
alpine animals • 38
narwhals • 40
galápagos animals • 42
marsupials • 44
cave animals • 46

2
behavior

habitats • 50
bird nests • 52
communication • 54, 56
symbiosis • 58
grooming • 60
migration • 62
hibernation • 64
tools • 66
beehives • 68
ant colonies • 70
bioluminescence • 72

Best foot forward *Showing off his moves, a male blue-footed booby (Sula nebouxii), right, prances for a female in the Galápagos Islands. A booby's courting dance often includes a high-stepping strut to show off his feet*

3
reproduction
mating rites • 76, 78
courting rites • 80, 82
parenting • 84, 86
marsupial parenting • 88
play • 90
fish reproduction • 92
metamorphosis • 94
seeds • 96
pollination • 98
fungi • 100

4
feeding
raptors • 104
hunting strategies • 106
predators • 108
spiderwebs • 110
carnivorous plants • 112
defensive strategies • 114
camouflage • 116, 118
color-changing animals • 120

Introduction
Planet of Wonders

A BUTTERFLY WITH TRANSPARENT WINGS! SCIENTISTS AND lepidopterists may be familiar with *Greta oto*, but to many readers, the existence of the "clearwing" or "glasswing" butterfly may come as a delightful surprise. This specimen was photographed in a cloud forest—a mountainous, fog-shrouded rain forest—in Costa Rica. Its see-through wings belie another, deadly surprise: the caterpillar from which it sprang fed on a toxic nightshade plant, and its natural predators have learned through bitter experience that the adult butterfly retains that toxicity.

The story of this single creature encompasses many of the themes of this book: the adaptation of species to their specific ecosystems; nature's eternal, deadly dance between predator and prey; the fascinating ways in which animals and plants reproduce and mature—in this case, through the exotic process of metamorphosis, in which an animal inhabits two entirely different types of body in its progress through this world. Above all, in its sheer, surprising beauty, the glasswing butterfly reflects the central message of this book: that Planet Earth is teeming with wonders, if we take the time to explore them.

In recent years the imperiled state of our planet has offered far more cause for concern than wonder. News of the natural world has focused on animals threatened by climate change or habitat loss or disease, such as the alarming decline in the world's honeybee population caused by a puzzling new syndrome, colony collapse disorder. This is as it should be, for the state of the planet is one of the most challenging problems of our time. Yet however essential, such reports can divert us from savoring the sheer fecundity, diversity, beauty and, yes, oddity, of the plants and animals of this remarkable planet.

So while this book reports on the latest scientific research into the subjects it covers, it is not intended to be a textbook or encyclopedia of the natural world. Rather, it is intended as a journey of discovery, inviting readers to enjoy the surprise and delight to be found in a wide-ranging exploration of the living wonders of our planet. Share the thrill of scientists who are dissecting the first intact specimen of a colossal squid ever recovered. Smile as a beluga whale blows doughnut-shaped rings of air, just for fun. Marvel at the mimic octopus, which is so adept at imitating the look of other undersea creatures that it eluded scientific identification until the late 1990s. And wonder at the seeming magic by which a fuzzy, crawling caterpillar blossoms into a butterfly whose wings are as clear as glass and as toxic as a nightshade plant. ∎

—*The Editors*

All clear? *A glasswing butterfly,* Greta oto, *alights on the branch of a fern in Costa Rica*

adaptation

*In this broad Earth of ours,
Amid the measureless grossness and the slag,
Enclosed and safe within its central heart,
Nestles the seed Perfection.*

—Walt Whitman, *Song of the Universal*

Hiding place *This Andean marsupial treefrog (Gastrotheca riobambae) is a baby, only two weeks removed from its tadpole days. He takes refuge in the hollow of a bromeliad flower in Ecuador*

rain-forest birds

A Paradise of Plumage

RAIN FORESTS ARE NATURE'S AVIARIES: A representative 4-sq.-mi. (10.3 sq km) swath of tropical jungle may contain up to 400 species of birds, and 1 of every 5 birds on the planet is believed to live in the Amazon rain forest alone. Indeed, birds are essential to the survival of the rain forest. Fruit-eating species like toucans soar and swoop hundreds of miles through the canopy, carrying seeds great distances from the parent tree. Research published in the late 1990s reported that three breeds of hornbill alone were the prime agents in the seeding of a quarter of all tree species within the rain forests of Cameroon.

The striking coloration of many tropical birds is driven largely by the need to attract mates. But the iridescent plumage is also a product of the birds' environment: although parrot feathers stand out like a rainbow to human eyes in the light of day, these colors behave differently in the muted, indirect light beneath a rain-forest canopy, especially in the perception of other animals, which see fewer colors than humans. Sadly, the bold plumage of rain-forest birds also attracts the attention of humans, who are willing to pay thousands of dollars to own them as exotic pets. And this, given the reliance of the rain forests on birds to spread the seeds of their flora, is bad news for more than just the birds. ∎

Jungle Kaleidoscopes
The 7.5-in. (19 cm) bill of a Toco toucan (Ramphastos toco), shown in Brazil on the facing page, appears large enough to make the bird top-heavy, but it is actually light and spongy.

Above, a male Raggiana bird of paradise (Paradisaea raggiana) struts his stuff for a prospective mate in Papua New Guinea.

At left top, the Sulawesi red knobbed hornbill (Aceros cassidix) is a monogamous species that thrives in tropical forests.

The resplendent quetzal (Pharomachrus mocinno), bottom left, is widely considered the most beautiful bird on the planet; it was regarded as a deity by the Maya and Aztecs.

rain-forest plants

Orchids
There are some 300 varieties of orchid in the genus Odontoglossum; *the beauties at left,* Odontoglossum crispum, *are native to the rain forests of Colombia. Almost all orchids are epiphytes, plants that grow by attaching themselves to other plants; since these "air plants" need not root in soil, they can grow high in the forest canopy, where there is more sunlight.*

Rafflesia
Sorry, Texans: the largest flower in the world, Rafflesia arnoldii, *is native to the South Pacific.* Rafflesia *are parasitic plants that nourish themselves from a host vine; their largest flowers can be more than 3.2 ft. (100 cm) in diameter and weigh up to 22 lbs. (10 kg). The flower emits a very foul odor; it was named for the Briton who founded Singapore (and is the eponym of its famous hotel), Sir Thomas Raffles.*

Bromeliads

This group of tropical and subtropical plants is so diverse, it includes both Spanish moss and pineapples. Bromeliads are distinguished by their stiff leaves and a central flower stem that often forms a receptacle that traps rainwater, providing a vital source of nourishment for many tropical animals. Most bromeliads are native to the Americas.

Lianas

Rain forests are so dense with vegetation that survival of the fittest becomes survival of the tallest. With precious sunlight dim on the forest floor, it's the plants highest in the canopy that thrive, so climbing vines plant their roots in the soil, then hitch a ride on trees to send their leaves toward the sun. Such climbers are called lianas, a name that identifies not a specific plant but rather all vines that grow vertically.

 amphibians

Charming

MANY PEOPLE CLAIM TO DISLIKE FROGS, and we stigmatize them as charming princes under an evil spell in our fairy tales. But it's still hard not to smile at the two-toned, long-fingered fellow at right. Amphibians don't get much more adorable or much more resplendent than the small frogs of the rain forest, whose vivid hues are a match for the colorful birds and flowers of the tropics—as well as a warning to predators, for many frogs secrete poisons from their skin.

If slime is a crime, rain-forest frogs are guilty, as are their relatives in the class Amphibia: newts and salamanders, toads and bullfrogs. Their skin is designed to be slimy and clammy; subdermal mucous glands keep it moist, as do the humid, wet places they call home: ponds, marshes, swamps and rain forests. For amphibians are creatures equally at home in two worlds, the watery hydrosphere and the solid pedosphere. Indeed, the life cycle of many amphibians recapitulates the long history of this group of sea creatures that adapted to life on dry land. Frogs, for example, begin their lives as tadpoles in the aquatic world, breathing through gills, then undergo a dramatic metamorphosis: their bodies develop arms, legs and lungs, and they emerge as terrestrial, air-breathing adults. Most of these cold-blooded vertebrates reproduce externally, with the male and female expelling sperm and unfertilized eggs at the same time. In some cases the parents guard the eggs until the larvae are fully developed.

In recent years amphibians have made news, but not for their charm. An ongoing study by the Global Amphibian Assessment group found that a total of 1,896 species—some 32 percent of the more than 5,900 known species of all known amphibians—are now considered highly endangered. Global climate change that is reducing and altering habitats, as well as the newly discovered fungal disease chytridiomycosis, are the twin engines that are driving this potentially irreversible decline in biodiversity. ∎

Peekaboo! *A splendid leaf frog* (Agalychnis calcarifer) *surveys his moist domain. Yes, splendid is part of his name*

 reptiles

Respect Your Elders

At home in deserts and tundra, in marshes, rain forests and a few watery habitats as well, reptiles make up an enormous clan of loosely related creatures, all of which share a handful of defining characteristics. All reptiles are cold-blooded: they cannot regulate their own body temperature by metabolic means, forcing them to achieve a suitable temperature through behavior or habitat. All reptiles breathe with lungs rather than gills, and all share a distinguished heritage; they are descended from ancient, four-limbed amphibian animals. Scientists believe their paths diverged some 340 million years ago. The reptile family tree leads directly to dinosaurs (and thus to birds); today's reptiles are closely related to the long-extinct dinosaurs, whose name means "terrible lizard."

Some reptiles, like snakes, became limbless, slithering creatures. The majority, however, retain four limbs that end in claws. Most reptiles reproduce by laying eggs: some abandon their brood seconds after depositing them, others incubate their eggs, and still others care for their young. The extended reptile family includes lizards, turtles and tortoises, as well as crocodiles and alligators, a total of more than 8,000 separate species. The class Reptilia is so disparate that a few seeming look-alikes have almost no connection to each other. Crocodiles and lizards bear a family resemblance, for example, but crocs are, genetically speaking, more closely related to birds than to lizards.

Despite their diversity and heritage, reptiles get a bum rap. Humans instinctively fear them; some biologists believe this is an evolutionary holdover, for long ago, the only predators able to reach baby primates in trees were snakes. Scaly and cold, reptiles often play the villain in stories and films, including, of course, that evergreen best seller, the Book of Genesis. ∎

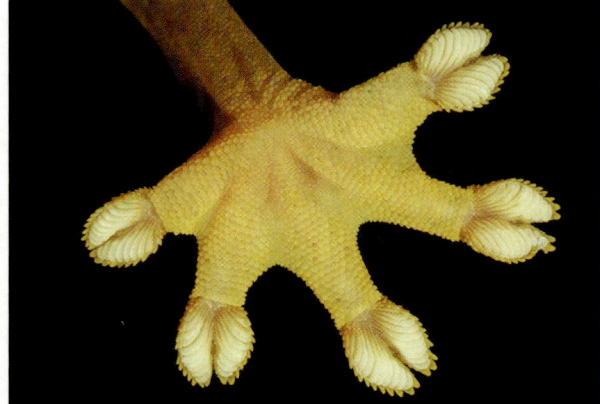

Reptile Fashion: Frills, Scales, Shells and Sticky Feet
Although all reptiles have scaly, protective skins, tortoises and turtles like the ornate box turtle (Terrapene ornata), at far left, are the only members of the group that have shells.

Many reptiles are adapted to specific environments: the giant leaf-tailed gecko (Uroplatus fimbriatus) in Madagascar, above, seems to be showing off that it has 300 teeth— more than any other land animal—to help it capture frogs and other small, slippery animals. Other reptiles attract mates or deter predators by flashing dewlaps, fans or frills, such as the frill-necked lizard (Chlamydosaurus kingii), at left, assuming a defensive posture in Australia's Outback.

Leaf-tailed geckos, like most lizards, are adept climbers, for the scales of their oversized feet are covered with microscopic adhesive bristles too tiny to be seen even in the close-up above.

desert plants

Brief Lives

DESERTS AREN'T NECESSARILY DESERTED. WHILE THE Sahara, Gobi and Arabian deserts resemble oceans of sand, semiarid deserts, like those of the U.S. Southwest, are bursting with plants adapted to surviving on 10 to 20 in. (25 to 50 cm) of rainfall a year: hundreds of species of trees, bushes, lilies, orchids and, of course, cacti (13 kinds) thrive here. Desert plants adapt to challenges—too much sunlight, not enough rain—in three ways: by hoarding water, going to sleep or, well, living fast and dying young.

Plants that accumulate water are succulents, and cacti are the best-known example of this group. The root systems of these hoarders are wide but shallow, so they can quickly capture the maximum amount of water from infrequent desert rains, which they can store for decades, if necessary.

Plants that sleep through long periods without water only to awake and thrive after a shower, like the creosote bush, are called "drought dormant." Deeper roots help them continue to draw moisture long after a rain shower ends. During dry spells, such plants enter a comalike state, during which metabolic activity comes to a near standstill, and their rate of photosynthesis slows.

But the oddest survival strategy of desert plants involves living briefly. "Drought avoidant" plants mature in a single growing season—often in autumn, when the mercury falls and the rains begin—and expend their resources on creating very hardy seeds that will sprout the following year or several years later, when adequate moisture is present. These desert "annuals" (or, more accurately, "ephemerals") make up half the plant life in some deserts, creating the explosive displays of spectacular wildflower blooms that light up the rugged landscape for a few weeks each year. In the desert, beauty and brevity walk hand-in-hand. ∎

Plants of the Semiarid Desert

Arizona's Organ Pipe Cactus National Monument, above, is filled with Mexican golden poppies, short cholla cacti and tall, long-armed saguaro cacti, water hoarders than can take up to 75 years to grow a single branch.

At far left, a barrel cactus grows small fruit buds that are shaped like pineapples and taste like lemons. At center, the queen of the night cactus conserves moisture by blossoming in darkness. At near left and right: two views of prickly pear cacti in the Chihuahuan Desert; these succulents spread themselves horizontally to collect water efficiently.

desert animals

Namaqua Chameleon
Lizards are one of the largest groups of reptiles, with some 5,000 species found in various ecosystems around the world. Like Chamaeleo namaquensis *at left, these cold-blooded, usually small, critters (excepting the large Komodo dragon, or monitor) are well adapted to life in scorching deserts. Along with snakes, lizards form the order Squamata, reptiles that are distinguished by their scaly skins.*

Mexican Red Knee Tarantula
Yes, these arachnids are big and hairy, and many folks find them scary. But the toxic bite of Brachypelma smithi *and other members of the family Theraphosidae is more irritating than deadly to humans. Even so, these spiders are big enough to prey on lizards, mice and even birds. They are at home in hot climes, including semiarid deserts and tropical forests.*

Coyote
Canines are among the most adaptable of species: dogs, wolves and their kin prosper in almost every ecosystem on land. The coyote, Canis latrans, *is at home in the desert but can range as far north as just below the Arctic Circle. Coyotes dwell only in the Americas; they are among the most vocal of wild mammals, using several distinct calls for greeting, warning, claiming territory and noting their location.*

Thorny Devil
British zoologist John Edward Gray christened this 8-in. (20 cm)-long lizard that roams Australia's Outback Moloch horridus, *evoking the Old Testament's horrid god of sacrifice. Aussies followed suit with a common name that hits the scale on the head, for this reptile protects himself from predators by making himself as unappetizing as possible, sporting tough ridges upon his entire body that end in two devilish horns on his head.*

grassland animals

Beat it! *Watering holes on Africa's vast grassland, the Serengeti plain, can be models of democracy, as zebras, elephants, antelope and birds share a drink in peace. But some species are not meant to mingle: even the Serengeti's apex predator, the lion, beats a retreat when a far larger mammal butts in*

grassland animals

Okapi
Once known as "forest zebras" because of their striped rumps, okapi (Okapia johnstoni) are related to giraffes but prefer more forested terrain than giraffes, which are more at home in grasslands. These hoofed mammals are vegetarians; their long, prehensile tongues help them gather the 40-65 lbs. of twigs, leaves, grass and fruit they eat each day. Okapis are now found only in the forests of the Democratic Republic of Congo.

Springbok
Demonstrating how it earned the first part of its name, this springbok (Antidorcas marsupialis) *is showing off its flair at stiff-legged pronking—leaping vertically into the air. Scientists posit this behavior is meant to distract potential predators. The antelope can pronk more than 10 ft. (3 m) into the air.*

Spotted Hyena
Famed as Africa's best scavengers, spotted hyenas (Crocuta crocuta) *have very strong jaws—and strong stomachs that can digest parts of animals others cannot. Like owls, they regurgitate indigestibles such as hooves, hair and ligaments in condensed pellets. These highly social animals are expert hunters that prefer to stalk their prey in a group, or clan.*

Common Warthog
It's not among nature's prettiest critters; indeed, the common warthog (Phacochoerus africanus) *is set apart by three sets of facial warts, and both males and females sport two long tusks. Hitching a ride here is a symbiotic bird that dines on parasites, the yellow-billed oxpecker* (Buphagus africanus).

shorebirds

Hanging on *Like many shorebirds, this little egret* (Egretta garzetta) *in Africa is losing some of its habitats to human settlement, but it is not considered endangered*

snakes like the diamondback rattler above are among the animal kingdom's most efficient killers. Snake venoms are some of the deadliest toxins found in nature, and experiments have shown that some snakes can estimate the amount of poison needed to kill a given victim and adjust a fatal dose accordingly.

Rattlesnakes are members of the family Viperidae, a widely dispersed type of venomous snake that is common in North and South America and across eastern Europe and Asia. The rattles in its tail are modified scales that assume the form of hollow beads nested within one another. Rattlers shed their skin several times a year, growing a single new bead each time.

An estimated 8,000 people are bitten by venomous snakes annually in the U.S., but fewer than 14 deaths due to snakebites are recorded in a typical year, thanks to the development of antivenin, which counteracts the anti-blood-clotting agents in the rattler's venom. ■

coral reefs

Creatures of the Reef

MEASURED BY VOLUME, CORAL REEFS DON'T amount to much: they take up only 1% of the planet's ocean floor. By almost every other yardstick, however, they are vitally important. Home to some one-quarter of all underwater species, coral reefs are a delicate and wondrously beautiful ecosystem in which thousands of different life-forms cooperate for mutual benefit. The symbiotic creatures that create such reefs—the coral polyp and the tiny algae called zooxanthellae that take refuge inside them and, in return, pass nutrients to their host—fertilize plant life around the reef, attracting tiny fish that graze on seaweed and other aquatic flora. These, in turn, lure larger fish that prey on them. The result is an iridescent underwater city, teeming with life and activity. Here urban sprawl is welcome: as one generation of coral dies, its offspring expand the 'hood by building new shells on top of their parents' skeletons.

Sponges, Clams and Corals
Like all sponges, the large orange Latrunculia magnifica *at left, photographed in the Red Sea, is a primitive animal that filters nutrients from the sea for food. Not all corals have hard exoskeletons: at top above are free-standing mushroom leather corals, with polyps extended in feeding mode. At bottom, a giant clam,* Tridacna gigas, *expels a cloud of eggs. The largest bivalve mollusk, a giant clam can be more than 3 ft. (1 m) across and weigh more than 400 lbs. (181 kg). Like most corals, giant clams are host to algae that provide nourishment; they also filter nutrients from the sea. Sadly, ripping yarns that such undersea behemoths are capable of eating humans are, in Mark Twain's term, "stretchers."*

Sometimes called the rain forests of the sea, coral reefs are to the oceans what forests are to continents: sanctuary and breeding ground for fish and plant species that will disappear without them. Parrotfish, spiny lobsters, shrimp, urchins, sea snakes and billowy squid are among the colorful species that rely on these underwater colonies. Like rain forests, coral reefs are also natural pharmacies, from which numerous beneficial drugs have been derived.

There is another compelling reason why coral reefs play an outsized role in the life of another species with which they share the planet: their nooks and crannies accommodate fish and shellfish that are important sources of food and livelihood for millions of human beings. In short, if these undersea living wonders die off, many humans may perish along with them. ∎

crustaceans

Hermit Crab
These 10-legged crustaceans, members of the superfamily Paguroidea, are not true crabs, but they are similar to cave-dwelling hermits, for they live inside the castoff shells of such gastropods as marine snails and retreat inside them when danger is near. A hermit crab will call a number of different-sized shells home as it grows larger.

Hinge-Beak Shrimp
This striped fellow, Rhynchocinetidae durbanensis, has the key traits of the arthropod phylum, which includes insects, arachnids, crustaceans and such myriapods as centipedes: a segmented body encased in a hard exoskeleton. Most crustaceans are aquatic and have two pairs of antennae and compound eyes that rest on stalks.

Ghost Crab
The large eyes mounted on stalks serve Ocypode quadrata *well; they give it 360° vision with which to hunt insect prey. But it is blind overhead, so it prefers to burrow into the sand to escape becoming birdfood. The amphibious crustacean leaves its shore burrow at night to take on oxygen as water washes over its gills; it also spawns in the ocean. While it may look fierce, it's only a few inches wide.*

Bullseye Reef Lobster
Why the name? Note the target on the right side of Enoplometopus holthuisi. *Lobsters are the largest crustaceans and are distinguished for their long, adept claws—pincers and crushers—which they use to crack open the shells of their favorite foods, mussels, clams, starfish and crabs.*

sea creatures

Bluespotted Ribbontail Ray
Its common name describes Taeniura lymma *well but fails to capture its unearthly beauty. Rays are flat because they are adapted to life close to the seabed, and most of them bury themselves partially under the sand of the ocean floor to surprise their prey. Like many rays, the bluespotted ribbontail has a barbed spine that protrudes from its posterior. The "winged" wonder feeds on crabs, shrimps and mollusks.*

Pacific Sea Nettle
Most sea nettles, a type of stinging jellyfish, are found in Atlantic waters, but this one lives in the Pacific Ocean. It is a cnidarian, a phylum of aquatic animals that includes sea anemones and coral. Chrysaora fuscescens is carnivorous; stinging tentacles help it trap and eat plankton, minnows and worms. Its mouth is on the underside of its body, or "bell," amid the tentacles.

 sea creatures

Scalloped Hammerhead Shark

This specimen of Sphyrna lewini *was photographed off the Galápagos Islands. Both this deadly predator's eyes and its nostrils are at the tips of the flattened projection on its snout. The unusual hammerhead shape provides lift for the animal and also increases its sensory capabilities, helping it find prey more easily. Sharks are among the oldest living advanced creatures on the planet; far older than dinosaurs, they pre-date the appearance of vertebrates on land.*

Guineafowl Puffer

The comically tiny fins of the pufferfish don't provide much propulsion to escape predators, so Arothron meleagris relies on two other mechanisms to avoid stalkers. First, it inflates its elastic stomach with water (or air), swelling up to a size that may make a predator think twice about attacking. Second, it possesses one of the deadliest toxins, tetrodotoxin, in the animal kingdom. The lethal fish is famously prized as sushi in Japan—once the chef has carefully removed its toxic parts.

deep-sea fish

Fangtooth

How Low Can You Go?

A WORLD OF UTTER DARKNESS, SEVERE cold and enormous pressure, the deep ocean is one of the planet's harshest biospheres. It is only in recent decades that scientists have begun to explore this hidden realm, yet they have been surprised to find that a number of creatures have adapted themselves to survive in this challenging environment.

The fish that dwell in this stark world boast some highly effective adaptations: many are bioluminescent, bringing their own light to these dark spaces. Some extend lures that are part of their anatomy; some have enormous jaws that allow them to scoop up prey even larger than themselves; some have strong fins that serve as legs, propelling them across the bottom of the ocean. Probably as a result of the severe pressures of the deep waters, most are rather small: the fangtooth above is scary to behold, but it tops out at 6 in. (15 cm) in length. As they continue to probe life in the depths, scientists believe there are many more species of deep-sea fish yet to be discovered. ∎

Anglerfish

Anglerfish

Gulper

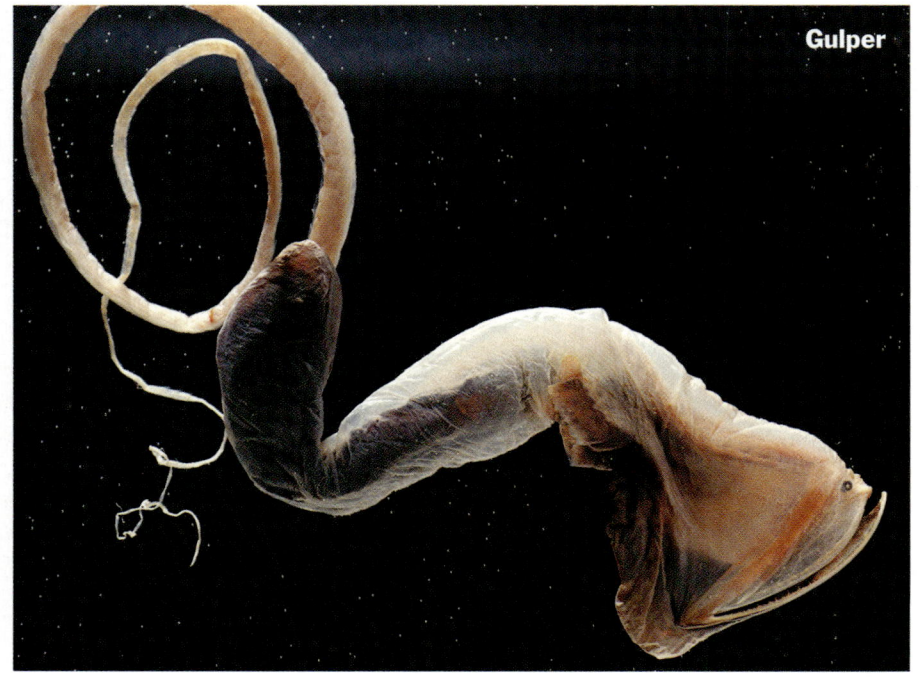

Deep Throats

Fangtooth (Anoplogaster cornuta). *This ugly fish has been found as far as 16,400 ft. (5,000 m) under the waves. Its two giant bottom fangs fit into deep sockets on its top jaw.*

Anglerfish (Gigantactis vanhoeffeni). *This fish has a projecting "fishing rod" off its forehead that ends in a bioluminescent "lure" that attracts small prey.*

Gulper (or Swallower) (Saccopharynx lavenbergi). *This relative of the eel has a mouth that opens so wide it can eat prey larger than itself. It lives at depths of 10,000 ft. (3,048 m).*

Anglerfish (genus Linophryne). *An inflated epidermis helps the larval stage of the fish stay buoyant until it matures.*

squid

A Colossal Discovery

It's official: sea monsters are real. At least the colossal squid is real. This octopus-like cephalopod, as long as a school bus, has been spoken of in hushed whispers by mariners since Homer wrote of the many-tentacled Scylla in *The Odyssey*. In the centuries since, most scholars dismissed the colossal squid as a myth. Yet as of April 2008, the first specimen of the species ever recovered whole and then frozen, a female, was lying in a New Zealand laboratory, slowing thawing out.

Scientists have been reasonably sure since 1925 that a cephalopod predator even larger than the giant squid (genus *Architeuthis*), shown above, roams the deep. That's when a sperm whale was cut open whose stomach contained two tentacles far larger than those of even the biggest known giant squid. In the years since, the stomachs of other sperm whales have been found to contain numerous razor-sharp beaks that were similarly too large for giant squids. But the only

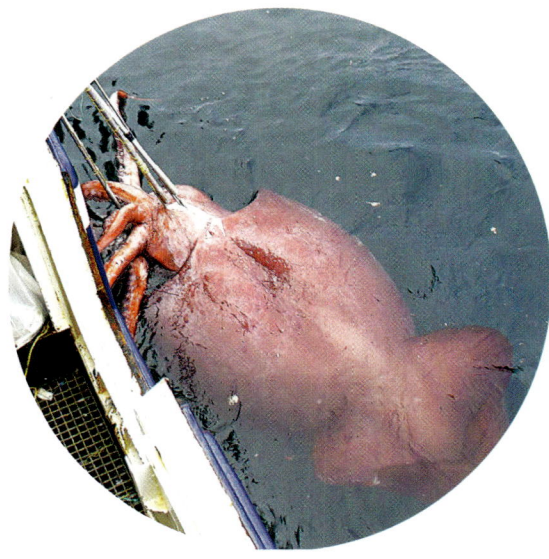

An Unexpected Catch

At left, a giant Humboldt squid (Dosidicus gigas) *is photographed in all its weird glory. The tentacled, beaked, deep-sea invertebrate moves by jet power, pushing seawater through its torso, or mantle, and expelling it from its posterior to provide thrust.*

Above, a deceased female colossal squid, the first recovered whole, is brought aboard the New Zealand fishing trawler San Aspiring *on Feb. 22, 2007, in the Ross Sea in Antarctica. Amid their more serious investigations of the creature, scientists at New Zealand's national museum, Te Papa Tongarewa, also satisfied their curiosity about a more personal point as they dissected the creature: they cooked a small sample of the colossal squid and ate it. Their verdict? "Delicious."*

specimens of the colossal squid, *Mesonychoteuthis hamiltoni*, ever caught appeared to be merely big kids: these immature specimens were about the same size as a fully grown giant squid. That changed in 2007, when an intact, mature colossal squid was netted by fishermen off the coast of Antarctica and quickly frozen. It turned out to be 34 ft. (10 m) long and weighed more than 1,000 lbs. (454 kg). What's more, that female may be a comparative midget: scientists estimate that colossal squid can grow to be some 46 ft. (14 m) long.

Forensic examination, ongoing in 2008, showed that the jumbo mollusk is the largest invertebrate on Earth and has the biggest eyes of any creature on the planet: the size of basketballs, each has a pupil as wide as an orange. Colossal squid are believed to be highly aggressive, even attacking their chief predators, sperm whales, and leaving deep gouges on the backs of the whales, battle scars never before explained. ■

penguins

Torpedoes in Tuxedos

BRILLIANTLY ADAPTED TO THEIR HARSH POLAR environment, penguins are among the planet's most fascinating animals: they breed like birds, swim like fish, socialize like humans, dress like dandies and share the joie de vivre of the playful otter family. Like all birds, they boast feathers and lay eggs, but these flightless creatures spend as much as 75% of their lives in the water. So the forelimbs that would function as wings for other birds have been transformed into flippers, while their feathers are so tightly packed (as many as 75 quills per square inch) that they resemble leathery skin. Their coats are "countershaded" to conceal them from ocean predators: jet-black backs blend in with the watery depths when seen from above, while white bellies disappear into the bright surface of the ocean when seen from below. And their bodies have evolved into the hydrodynamic torpedo shape seen in water animals from beavers to whales. Like beavers, penguins move clumsily on land, but these superb swimmers dart through the water at up to 15 m.p.h. (24 km/h). Some species of penguin may swim as far as 3,000 miles (5,000 km) between feeding

Bombs away! *Emperor penguins dive into Antarctic waters, seeking the fish, squid, octopus and krill that make up their diets*

grounds and nesting areas, on voyages that last for many months. Monitoring devices reveal that emperor penguins—at 4 ft. (1.2 m) tall, the largest species—sometimes dive as deep as 1,700 ft. (518 m) and can stay underwater for up to 11 minutes.

All penguins live south of the equator, ranging from the Antarctic to as far north as the Galápagos Islands. Highly social creatures, they engage in elaborate rituals, such as bill-jousting and flipper-boxing, as they fight over mates. They have even developed a form of currency with the pebbles they use to build nests. Females will sometimes steal pebbles from one another's piles, and males of some species bow and present their mates with a pebble before breeding. Mates also bond by touching necks and slapping one another's backs. When pebbles are scarce, some females "sell" sex in exchange for the stones needed to build a nest. After chicks are born, all the parents from a colony will sometimes engage in a celebratory display in which they thump their chests with their flippers while leaning their heads back and crowing loudly. Monitoring devices have not yet detected the presence of cigars. ∎

alpine animals

Snow Leopard
We may think of leopards as animals of the jungles and plains, but heavy-furred Panthera uncia *is native to the mountains of central Asia. A bit smaller than other species of leopard, it is admired for its lovely coat of white fur dappled with spots. Unlike most of the other big cats, the snow leopard cannot roar.*

Musk Ox
There's a reason Ovibos moschatus *is known as the musk ox; males give off a strong odor in rutting season, when they also butt heads for mating rights. These long-horned bovines with shaggy winter coats were hunted almost to extinction and now are found only in northern Canada and the Arctic Circle.*

Ermine
The small mammal is prized by humans for its blinding-white winter coat, seen here on a specimen in the Alps. Ermines (Mustela erminea) *are close relatives of ferrets, weasels and minks; they are all members of the family Mustelidae, small carnivorous mammals that have short legs and long bodies.*

Snow Monkey
High in the mountains of Japan's Honshu Island, these Japanese macaques, or snow monkeys (Macaca fuscata), *are blissing out in the Jigokudani hot spring in Nagano, site of the 1998 Winter Olympics. The monkeys can withstand extreme winter cold, but they are also at home in temperate forests.*

narwhals

Tusk-ans *The unicorns of the sea, narwhals (Monodon monoceros) are members of the order Cetacea, along with whales, dolphins and porpoises. Unlike baleen whales, which filter small prey from the water, narwhals are toothed whales that feed on small fish. Male narwhals grow a distinctive single tusk, though some female narwhals have one. Males appear to "fence" with their tusks at times, an activity that was once viewed as a mating duel but may be a means of cleaning the spears.*

Narwhals are found only in the Arctic. Above, the aquatic mammals gather in an ice break to breathe. At right, the tusks grow in a clockwise spiral and can reach almost 10 ft. (3 m) in length; narwhals themselves are 23 to 26 ft. (7 to 8 m) in length

 galápagos animals

Smoke signals *The Galápagos tortoise gave the islands their name; the word is taken from the Spanish term for "saddle," which their shells resemble. The smoking fumaroles in the background are a reminder that the archipelago is still geologically active*

Alternate Bestiaries

SIX MILLION YEARS AGO, ALONG THE EASTERN EDGE of the Pacific Ocean's Ring of Fire, a string of undersea volcanoes poked above the waves, blew their tops, then lapsed into a prolonged, if restless, sleep. The dozen-plus islands that remained were almost 600 miles (960 km) from the nearest landmass and were left undiscovered by humans until 1535, when a Panamanian cleric's ship was blown off course on his way to Peru. In the meantime, however, thousands of other accidental tourists found the Galápagos. Lost birds alighted there and never left. Small land animals blown out to sea floated there on "rafts" of leaves and timber. Spores and seeds were borne to the islands on the breeze. As soon as they arrived, all these fauna and flora began to be shaped by their new environment. The result was (and is) a living laboratory of what happens to plants and animals in complete isolation—cut off not only from human interference, but also from the competition and predation of other species.

The islands' most famous visitor discovered in the Galápagos a new Eden: an environment where almost half the plants, nearly all the reptiles and many of the other animals were unique—found nowhere else on the planet. "Both in space and time, we seem to be brought somewhat near to that mystery of mysteries, the first appearance of new beings on earth," Charles Darwin wrote in 1835. The British biologist noticed that among more than a dozen species of finches found only on the Galápagos, each had a differently shaped beak, uniquely suited to its own food source. This observation, "seemed to me to throw some light on the origin of species," Darwin wrote later, coining the phrase that would become the title of his epochal treatise on natural selection.

Generations of later scientists also benefited, like Darwin, from another unique feature of the Galápagos environment: animals that have never been preyed upon don't have the fight-or-flight instinct that makes direct observation of wildlife so challenging elsewhere. Even now, birds, lizards and nearly every other creature on the Galápagos Islands are as tame and unafraid of humans as golden retrievers.

Today, the islands are famed for their native species, which include the giant Galápagos tortoise, for whom the islands are named, the marine iguana and lava gulls, whose feathers match the color of the island's volcanic soil. And of course, for Darwin's finches and their probing, specialized, revelatory beaks. ∎

Galápagos Green Sea Turtle
Green sea turtles are found in abundance across the world, but this subspecies of Chelonia mydas, *endemic to the islands and prized for its meat, eggs and hide, is over-hunted and highly endangered. It is distinguished for its small size and relatively dark coloration.*

Marine Iguana
Amblyrhynchus cristatus *is the fellow on the bottom, and he's the world's only sea-going iguana. His friend is a lava lizard, genus* Tropidurus, *also found only in the Galápagos, in seven different species, each unique to its location in the archipelago.*

Nazca Booby
This sea-going bird, Sula granti, *is one of six booby species. It is found in the Galápagos and a few other locations in the eastern Pacific. The female lays two eggs, and the chick that hatches first shoves its sibling from the nest to die.*

marsupials

Offbeat mammals *Marsupials like the koala mother at left carry their infants in a pouch until they are fully formed, like this youngster. The process takes about six months. At near left is the only North American marsupial, the Virginia opossum, famed for its clever tactic of feigning death— "playing possum"—at a predator's approach. Opossums use their partially prehensile tails as a strong extra appendage*

G'day, Marsupials!

YOU MIGHT THINK OF MARSUPIALS AS MAMMALS viewed in a fun-house mirror. Like mammals, they give birth to live offspring and nurse their young. But their fascinating reproductive cycle, which involves the care of what is essentially an external embryo in the mother's abdominal pouch, sets them apart. Although kangaroos are the signature marsupial, the order Marsupialia is very diverse, numbering more than 200 species, including wombats, koala bears, bandicoots and Tasmanian devils. They range in size from southern dibblers a few inches long to kangaroos almost as tall as a human being. There are burrowing, grazing and hibernating marsupials, plant-eating and meat-eating marsupials. Some marsupials are tree-dwellers with pouches under their arms that help them glide for more than 100 ft. (30 m), in the same manner as a flying squirrel.

Marsupials and placentals (the dominant type of mammals, to which human beings belong) are thought to have diverged more than 100 million years ago, at a time when South America, Australia and Antarctica were still a single landmass. As the continents drifted apart, most marsupials in South America and all those in Antarctica died out, the former killed off by competition with hardier placentals, the latter unable to adapt to the harsh polar environment.

In Australia, where there were fewer placentals and a milder climate, marsupials not only dominated but became giants. Fossil records indicate that kangaroos twice as tall as humans and a wombat the size of a hippopotamus once roamed the Outback, as did marsupial lions with a bite stronger than any other creature that has ever lived.

While most of these mega-marsupials died off before the last Ice Age, the majority of the world's marsupial species are still endemic to Australia. The Tasmanian tiger, a close relative to the Tasmanian devil, was the largest carnivorous marsupial in the world, but it is believed to have died out in the 1930s. A few dozen species of marsupial continue to flourish in South America, but only a single marsupial, the Virginia opossum, still survives in North America. ■

cave animals

Hanging around *The large knob on the nose of this ghost bat* (Macroderma giga) *in a cave in northern Australia is called a nose-leaf: it is used in echolocation, a sort of sonar in which bats send out a series of clicking signals, then interpret their echoes to locate potential prey*

Cavern Critters

CAVES ARE STUDIES IN SEVERITY, SET APART among Earth's ecosystems by the absence of the natural riches that shape life on the planet's surface: there is little weather here, and the lack of sunlight rules out plants that flourish through photosynthesis. But if this subterranean world is long on minerals and short on vegetables, it is surprisingly rich in animals. Like other extreme zones—the poles, the deep sea, the desert—the stern necessities of the cave environment breed creatures so specifically adapted that they cannot exist elsewhere.

The absence of light exerts a profound impact on cave life. Many of the creatures here are blind, for eyes serve no purpose in a dark world. And since there is no light to illuminate colors, many cave-adapted creatures, like the crab and crayfish shown at right, are albinos. The lack of vegetation radically limits the diversity of species here: most cave animals are found in caverns where there is some fresh running water, providing a source of nourishment for fish, crabs, crayfish and other cavern-dwellers. Many creatures, such as wolves and bears, keep a foot in both worlds, maintaining dens in caves but frequently venturing outdoors to find sustenance.

The signature cave animal, the bat, is among those subterranean commuters. The winged mammals of the order Chiroptera are one of the planet's most diverse animals, with more than 900 distinct species. Bats are highly skilled predators, whose use of echolocation to find prey is one of nature's most efficient hunting adaptations. Highly sociable, bats roost by the thousands in caves across the world, though many species of bats also dwell in trees and cliffs. ∎

Troglobite or Troglophile?
Scientists call animals that dwell only in caves troglobites; their adaptations are troglomorphics. Among the most common of these adaptations is the absence of pigment, as seen in the crayfish and crab at left.

The salamander at top has plenty of pigment, but it is blind, as is the blind cave characin fish, a species of the Mexican tetra. Such animals are nourished by small creatures and vegetable matter found in freshwater streams and sometimes by bat guano. Bats and other animals that shuttle between caves and the surface world, like the cave salamander, are called troglophiles.

 behavior

*I think I could turn and live with animals, they are so placid
    and self-contain'd,
I stand and look at them long and long…*

*Not one is dissatisfied—not one is demented with the mania
    of owning things,
Not one kneels to another, nor to his kind that lived thousands
    of years ago
Not one is respectable or industrious over the whole earth.*
                      —Walt Whitman, *Song of Myself*

Patterns *During migrating season on Africa's Serengeti Plain, zebras* (Equus burchellii) *mingle freely with blue wildebeests* (Connochaetes taurinus)

habitats

Dig it! Meerkats are among the dozens of mammals that create homes by burrowing; others include groundhogs, moles and rabbits

Home, Sweet Home

HUMANS ARE FAR FROM THE ONLY ANIMALS THAT alter their environment by building homes for themselves. Spiderwebs, anthills, beehives and beaver dams all attest to the itch for engineering that seems hard-wired into the DNA of hundreds of species of animals. Even shrimp create their own habitats by burrowing into underwater rocks. Animal architects satisfy the same needs as human designers do: to protect young, attract mates, avoid predators, store food and provide shelter from the elements.

Nature's engineers may lack human intelligence and tools, but their creations are wonderfully diverse. At the bottoms of rivers and streams, the larvae of caddis flies capture passing silt, vegetation and even pebbles in a web of silk, then use them to encase themselves in a suit of armor that protects them from hungry fish and filters in water-borne nutrients. Other animals create dwellings of lavish intricacy. Multiple generations of badgers will add new rooms to their setts, sometimes bringing the total number of chambers to many dozens, and the elaborate burrows dug by some rats can have hundreds of entrances and exits. Paging Martha Stew-rat! ∎

Makeshift manor *The octopus at right has taken shelter with her eggs inside a glass jar beneath 50 ft. of water in Papua, New Guinea*

Monument *Anthills like this skyscraper in Australia's Northern Territory can reach impressive heights. Some fossilized anthills have been dated as millions of years old*

 bird nests

Bald eagles

Grosbeak weavers

Avian Architects

After human beings, birds may be nature's most sophisticated architects. They build nests that hang in the air, float on water and descend into the ground, as well as form the familiar "cup" design. To do so, they weave complicated knots, use sophisticated geometry, employ advanced chemistry and build elaborate disguises. So it's tempting, but misleading, to think of bird nests as the avian equivalent of human houses, the result of conscious planning.

In fact, bird nests are not true "homes." They usually serve only two temporary purposes, to protect eggs and raise youngsters, and are then abandoned. Nor does thought seem to be involved: experiments show that birds raised in captivity without ever seeing a nest will build precisely the kind their own species constructs in the wild when the nesting instinct calls.

Even so, bird engineering displays stunning range and complexity. A pair of bald eagles, one of the few species that return to the same nest each year, begins laying sticks in a triangular formation, then adds more layers above while rotating the triangle. The resulting structure can be more than 12 ft. (3.5 m) deep and weigh more than 2 tons. European starlings scavenge particular plants, like wild carrot and yarrow, whose chemical content checks the growth of parasites within the nest. And at least one species, the great crested flycatcher, adorns its nest with skin shed by a snake, to frighten off predators that savor birds but fear snakes.

Cowbirds don't build nests at all, for as parents, they practice abandonment and deceit: females stash their eggs in the nests of other species and let the adoptive parents hatch and raise their young. Slackers! ∎

White storks

Masked weaver

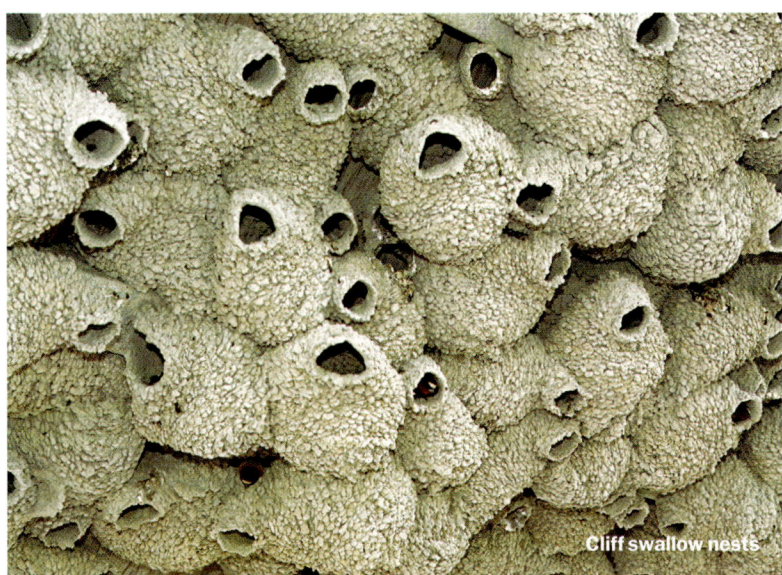

Cliff swallow nests

Wide World of Nests

Bald eagles (Haliaeetus leucocephalus), *shown here in Alaska, return to the same nest each season.*

Grosbeak weavers (Amblyospiza albifrons), *shown in a swamp on St. Lucia, are part of the passerine order, birds that build highly elaborate nests.*

White storks (Ciconia ciconia), *shown nesting on a rooftop in Austria, prefer to roost on man-made structures, like chimneys and barns.*

The lesser masked weaver (Ploceus intermedius), *shown here in South Africa, protects its young by building hanging nests, often above water, with entrance holes near the bottom.*

Cliff swallows (Hirundo pyrrhonota), *form communal nests from mud pellets cemented on cliffs or beneath overhangs.*

communication

Podcasts Dolphins, mankind's fellow mammals, are among the most social, playful and communicative of animals; this pod of Atlantic spotted dolphins (Stenella frontalis) was photographed swimming alongside a boat in the Azores. Like other cetaceans—whales and porpoises—dolphins have extremely acute hearing. These vociferous animals speak to one another using narrow-band whistles and by cackling and uttering sharp cries. They also issue high-pitched clicking sounds that are used for echolocation and may also be used for communication. Their voices are so distinctive that even humans can distinguish between individual dolphins

communication

Grizzly Bear   Orangutan

The Call of the Wild

WOLVES HOWL, LIONS GROWL, DOGS BARK, PORpoises click and birds sing, with whales joining in the chorus. The animal kingdom is abuzz with chatter. But what does it all mean? Animals communicate in ways that can be heard, seen, felt, even smelled, for many of the same reasons people do, especially on three subjects central to the continuation of life: food, sex and danger. Animals with voice boxes use their lungs to convey information with sound. Those lacking vocal equipment often make a racket with other body parts, ranging from the rattles of some snakes to the hind legs of crickets. Almost all the more complex animals have some means of exchanging signals with one another and with other species.

What's more, they often follow the patterns of human speech: low, guttural sounds seem mostly to refer to large objects and animals or are used to convey aggression. High-pitched noises most often connote smaller things, or imply submission.

But are any of these noises language? The frustrating answer appears to be "not exactly" in most cases, and "maybe" in at least one. Most animal vocalizations have meaning but lack what scientists call *syntax*. This term refers to the way in which humans combine words into phrases to convey a specific meaning and then switch them around to alter that meaning. For example, hundreds of animals are known to have an audible sign for danger, but not one has been found

Asian Elephant

Sperm Whale

Red Deer

to have a more complex signal like "danger coming from the top of the hill." Some species, though, come tantalizingly close: monkeys of the Ivory Coast sometimes qualify their "danger" noise with the equivalent of *maybe* when they are unsure of its source. And honeybees engage in an elaborate pattern of dances in which a forager pinpoints the range and direction (relative to the sun) of a newfound food source.

But most researchers say that even these sophisticated signals are more akin to a code than a true language. The animal that seems to come nearest to genuine language as humans know it is man's fellow mammal, the whale—with chatty, clicking porpoises close behind. Some researchers are convinced that whales imitate the sound of one another's voices and even compose songs that contain rhymes. Their long, complex arias have been shown via mathematical analysis to contain nonrandom groupings of sound that resemble the hierarchical structure of human phrasing. Like hippos, elephants, rhinos, pigeons and cuttlefish, whales also communicate in a way that people can't: they use "infrasound" (long-wave, low-frequency signals that cannot be detected by the human ear) to signal one another many miles away. The precise meaning of much animal conversation, however, still remains mysterious: to human ears, it is teasing but indecipherable, a mélange of sound and fury, signifying nothing. ∎

Our Mutual Friends

Every time you walk your dog or feed your cat, you are engaging in a symbiotic relationship. Although these creatures are valued today mainly for companionship, they were first domesticated by humans because dogs could provide security and help herd livestock, while cats could hunt vermin. In exchange for these benefits, the animals we think of as pets got a safe place to live and a steady supply of food. Derived from the Greek words for "living together," symbiosis is what happens when different species evolve a physically close, long-term relationship in which at least one party benefits. In most cases, such as the relationship between a parasite and its host, the second party is harmed in some way. In other symbioses, the second species is neither hurt nor helped. And in the kind of symbiosis best known to humans, the keeping of pets, both species derive profit from the exchange: this is called "mutualism."

One familiar example of mutualism unites the plant and animal kingdoms: bees, butterflies and birds derive sustenance from the flowers whose nectar they drink, even as they enable the flowering plants to reproduce by collecting and spreading their pollen. Nature is famously "red in tooth and claw," but cooperation in the form of symbiosis is one of its primary forces. Among the most striking examples of mutualism is agriculture—not the human kind, but the original version, invented by leaf-cutter ants around 50 million years ago. Around that time, the ants began chopping foliage into small pieces and carrying it down to their underground lairs. They did so not to eat the leaves, which are not part of their diet, but to cultivate a fungus that is the ants' primary food source. In the thousands of millennia since, the fungus has become so dependent on the ants for nutrition and security that its original reproductive organs have atrophied, and it now relies exclusively on being seeded and grown by ants to propagate itself.

Symbiosis often not only vaults the barriers dividing plants and animals but also transcends size. Human beings play host to legions of "gut flora" that live within our digestive tracts and help us process food. Sometimes, in fact, the relationship between symbiotic partners becomes so close and so useful that they merge into a single organism, or symbiont. Human beings may be among them: many scientists believe that the mitochondria that serve as the powerhouses for every cell in our bodies were once a separate species of symbiotic bacteria that were subsumed by their host organism (possibly a prehuman ancestor) and eventually became an inextricable part of us. In this sense, humans may be the ultimate symbionts. ■

Win-win situations *Four examples of symbiotic relationships: at left, both the impala and the red-billed oxpecker benefit when the latter eats ticks and flies from the former's hide. Above, from top to bottom: a marine iguana disposes of dead skin by sharing it with a sally lightfoot crab in the Galápagos; red-striped cleaner shrimp tidy up a moray eel's mouth in the Solomon Islands; and off the coast of Australia, a clown anemonefish takes shelter among the stinging tentacles of its sea anemone host, to whose poison it is impervious. In this protected "briar patch," the fish breeds and hides from predators. In turn, the clown fish drives predators away from the anemone*

 grooming

Cleaning Up Their Act

SOCIAL GROOMING AMONG ANIMALS IS A CLASSIC trade-off: "You scratch my back, and I'll scratch yours." Called allogrooming by scientists (as opposed to autogrooming, which is what happens, for example, when a cat licks itself clean), this behavior is seen in a surprising number of species, from bats and crabs to horses and wolves to primates and humans. Cooperative cleanliness offers animals three kinds of benefits: physical, mental and social. The primary advantage is that picking away parasites helps prevent disease. But grooming behavior is also known, at least in mammals, to trigger the release of endorphins, bringing on a state of relaxation and euphoria. When a pair of horses grooms each other, usually by nibbling at the back of the neck and on the withers, the heart rate of each animal slows down.

Finally, the entire community benefits when bonds between animals are strengthened. Chimps, for example, engage in celebratory orgies of grooming that last for hours when a member of their troop that has been away for an extended period of time rejoins the clan. Chimps also use grooming to steady their nerves after violent rampages by adult males. The urge to groom is so strong in some animals that it transcends the species barrier. Primates of different species that live together in zoos will sometimes groom one another, and each time a dog or cat affectionately licks its owner, it is bridging the same gap. A number of scientists have even proposed that grooming gave birth to language: University of Liverpool evolutionary biologist Robin Dunbar theorizes that as early human communities became too large for each member to establish a social connection with every other through touch, speech was devised as a means of accomplishing that goal. ∎

Shipshape *At top left, a knob-tailed gecko* (Nephrurus levis) *grooms itself, using its agile tongue to clear the grit of sand dunes from the lens of its lidless eye in Western Australia.*

Social grooming, or allogrooming, is a prominent behavior in primates; at top right, a family of drills (Mandrillus leucophaeus), *close relatives of baboons, searches each other's coats for parasites.*

At right, a colorful kingfisher (Alcedo atthis) *engages in preening, the term used for autogrooming in birds*

migration

On the move *A group of wildebeests fords the Mara River during migration in Kenya's Masai Mara National Reserve. In spring, these big antelopes move from the dry grasslands to the forest; they return in late fall, when rains turn the plains verdant again. Migration is a significant survival strategy for a wide variety of animals, including birds and undersea creatures as well as land animals, who would otherwise starve due to seasonal food shortages. Migrating in large groups helps wildebeests and other hoofed mammals that are easy prey for larger animals in two ways: it is less easy for predators to single out individuals from a pack, and there are more eyes, ears and noses to detect danger. For these wildebeests, the predator to be feared at the moment is in the river: crocodiles*

 hibernation

A Long Winter's Nap

ANIMALS THAT LIVE IN CLIMATES THAT VARY WITH the seasons employ three different strategies for dealing with cold weather and the food shortages it brings: bundle up, run away or go to sleep. Shrews and weasels choose Door No. 1: the former gorge themselves before winter, taking on a layer of insulation known as "brown fat," while the latter thicken their warm fur coats. Migratory creatures prefer the "run away" strategy, wintering where it's warmer. But for animals ill-equipped to eat so much or to travel so far, cold weather cues the big sleep.

Who's snoozing? Species of mice, skunks, raccoons, bats, frogs, turtles, snakes, snails and even some fish lapse in winter into a state of suspended animation, experiencing precipitous drops in body temperature (in many cases, close to freezing), while their heart rates slow to a few beats per minute. If removed from their shelters, many of these wild critters can be handled like toys for long periods without waking.

Bears are nature's best-known sleepyheads, yet most scientists don't classify them as true hibernators, because their body temperatures drop by only about 10° during their sleep, and they can be awakened with relative ease—if not without risk. But bears do perform a metabolic miracle that researchers have yet to understand: they stop expelling waste from their bodies and recycle the nitrogen content of urea, the usually poisonous primary component of urine, back into new protein. Bears not only lose fat during their winter sleep, as expected, but also, surprisingly, increase their lean tissue and bone mass.

Some creatures hibernate in summer: lungfish bury themselves in underwater mud and sleep for several months as their river homes run dry. This process, called estivation, comes full circle when they emerge from slumber with the autumn rains. ∎

Ready ... Set ... Doze
At top left, a black bear sow (Ursus americanus) *hibernates with her cub in Minnesota. Bears are light sleepers, even while hibernating, and can be dangerous if disturbed.*

At top right, garden snails (Helix aspersa) *cluster for winter in their hibernaculum, the zoological name for the place an animal chooses for its seasonal sleep.*

At right, a pair of dormice (Muscardinus avellanarius) *nap; the species is so well known for its annual hibernation that it takes its name from the French verb* dormir—"to sleep."

tools

Eureka!

WE THINK OF HUMANS AS TOOLMAKERS. But we are not alone: dozens of animals improvise implements, and in some cases actually fashion them, to manipulate their environments. Sea otters rest stones on their bellies and use them to crack open mussel shells; monkeys also use rocks to break nuts. Fire ants soak up water with moss sponges, then carry them back to help hydrate the colony. Bottlenose dolphins wrap sea sponges around their snouts to prevent cuts and scratches. Wild gorillas break off tree branches and employ them to test the depth of streams and rivers before wading in.

All these improvisations use materials readily at hand without changing their form. But do any animals actually make tools? Yes. Chimpanzees turn a stick into an insect catcher by stripping away its leaves and side branches, then breaking it into the right length before sliding it into a termite hole.

In the South Pacific, New Caledonian crows have been observed not only manipulating tools by bending a flexible material such as wire to reach around corners but also using multiple tools in succession. Scientists have also watched captive birds with a twig too short to reach a stash of food reject it and quickly grab another stick long enough to snag the meal. Birdbrains! ■

Bright Ideas
On the facing page, a brown capuchin monkey (Cebus apella) *uses a heavy rock "hammer" to crack open palm nuts it has placed in small pits on the surface of the larger rock "anvil."*

Twigs are often employed by animals as tools. At top of this page, a chimpanzee (Pan troglodytes) *at Washington Park Zoo feeds on insects it has fished out of their nest with a long stick. Above, a woodpecker finch* (Camarhynchus pallidus) *employs a cactus spine to extract grub from a dead tree in the Galápagos Islands.*

 beehives

Queen City

ONLY HALF OF WHAT MOST OF US THINK WE KNOW about honeybees is true: yes, these busy insects of the order Hymenoptera are highly specialized, with different members of their colony, the hive, focused exclusively on niche jobs like cleaning, building new rooms within the structure, regulating temperature and so on. But there is a surprising amount of freedom in bee-dom: most bees don't spend their entire lives devoted to only one of these jobs. Rather, they will rotate throughout their lives from one task to another.

The two exceptions to this rule are the queen, whose only job is to lay eggs, and the drones, males whose only job is to mate with Her Majesty. Each hive has only one queen and perhaps a few hundred drones, and for their entire lives these small minorities will be confined to their assigned roles. The rest of the hive's bees, as many as 50,000 workers—all of them females whose sexuality is deliberately undeveloped—share more than a dozen tasks, one of which is to remain at the entrance to the hive and beat their wings, so that the its unique scent will be fanned outward, helping guide other members home. Scientists describe such group-oriented creatures as eusocial—that is, beneficially communal. ■

No pension plan *Honeybees form the second most complex social organizations on the planet—after humans. Female honeybees climb a career ladder that progresses from jobs like housekeeping and feeding young to searching outside the hive for nectar and returning to process it to guarding the hive itself. In the process, they literally work themselves to death— buzzing around at up to 25 m.p.h., visiting as many as 10,000 flowers each day, carrying heavy loads of pollen and nectar back to the hive. At the end of their 40-to-50-day life spans, they either keel over from exhaustion or (unable to work anymore) are pushed out of the hive to starve or are stung to death by younger, more vigorous members. The same goes for drones and even the queen (the largest bee, above): all are killed when they can no longer contribute to communal life. Little wonder the Roman poet Virgil marveled at them, noting that they "pass their life under the might of the law"*

Come together *Honeybees* (Apis melifera) *form a chain as they work to repair the hive. Top left, a close-up of a bee's tongue as it laps up a sugar solution*

 ant colonies

Yellow-bellied *The hugely swollen abdomens of these honeypot ant repletes are suspended beneath their upper bodies in this Australian colony. At far left, an ant seeks sustenance from this communal "filling station"*

Priming the Pump

CALL IT COLONIALISM, INSECT DIVISION. THE globe swarms with more than 12,000 species of ants, whose colonies are found everywhere except Antarctica, Iceland, Greenland and a few South Pacific islands. And call it socialism: ant colonies survive only through the mutual assistance these intensely social insects provide to one another. A case in point is the honey ant: some species of this ant have evolved a specialized class of worker ant that stores vast amounts of food in its abdomen. But these treasures are not for personal use. Called "repletes," the ants suspend themselves from the ceiling of an underground nest, where they hang like light bulbs for weeks and months at a time. Early in their careers, repletes allow other members of the colony to approach and deposit food in their mouths. Later, after their abdominal cavities have swollen to the size of grapes, they permit their fellow colonists to make withdrawals from this communal food bank. No ant can share in a replete's larder, however, until it has identified itself with an elaborate series of coded antennae taps, certifying that it is a member of the same colony. In some species, the designated repletes are even more specialized, dividing themselves into separate niches to store nectar, insect juices and water.

Almost all ants play highly specialized roles within their colonies. Not only are they divided into broad castes like soldiers, hunter-gatherers and workers, but some species also break shared tasks down into minute, assembly-line jobs: leaf-cutter ants have distinct castes for processing foliage once it has been brought inside the nest. In other species, some workers are full-time custodians that carry debris to a "garbage dump" outside. A 2007 study from Warsaw's Jagiellonian University even suggests that ants can sense how much longer they have to live and then adjust their behavior accordingly: younger ants (whose loss would be a blow to the colony) are confined to safer tasks, while older ants (which will die soon, in any case) take on riskier jobs. "Go to the ant," King Solomon advises in the Old Testament. "Consider her ways and be wise." It's a rare monarch who lends his support to such a profoundly communistic society. ■

 bioluminescence

Let There Be Light!

"T**HE FIREFLY'S FLAME,**" OGDEN NASH DECLARED, "is something for which science has no name." But he was wrong: the technical term for the ability of living things to emit light is "bioluminescence," and it is found in thousands of different kinds of sea creatures, fungi and insects. Indeed, there are more than 2,000 different light-emitting species of fireflies, the blinking aviators that delight children on summer nights. Some plants also emit light: foxfire is a faint glow emitted by some species of mushrooms as they break down rotting wood.

Despite these examples, bioluminescence on land is comparatively rare. Where the tough really get glowing is where the sun never shines: in the ocean's mesopelagic zone. Here, in depths of roughly 600 to 3,300 ft. (183 to 1,006 m), as many of 90% of all aquatic flora are believed to create their own light. They range from shrimp to jellyfish to the bent-tooth bristlemouth, an unsung, glowing fish that may be the most abundant vertebrate on the planet. The ocean's tiniest inhabitants, such as plankton and bacteria, can even cause the sea itself to glow, as sometimes seen in California's famous "red tides" and in Bioluminescent Bay off the island of Vieques, Puerto Rico.

Why nature's *fiat lux*? Scientists are still debating this question, but the consensus is that bioluminescence serves at least one or more of four purposes: to scare off predators, lure prey, attract mates or communicate with others of the same species. Each firefly species has its own coded pattern of flashes that is recognized by prospective mates of the same breed.

Living lanterns switch on thanks to a quartet of agents. When a molecule called luciferin combines with an enzyme known as luciferase (both are named for Lucifer, whose name means "Light Bringer"), along with a cellular fuel known as adenosine triphosphate (ATP) in the presence of oxygen, light is released. One feature common to almost all bioluminescent life forms is their stunning efficiency. An ordinary light bulb squanders more than 90% of the energy it consumes by generating waste heat, but living light bulbs reverse this ratio—almost all the chemical energy they produce is used to create light. ■

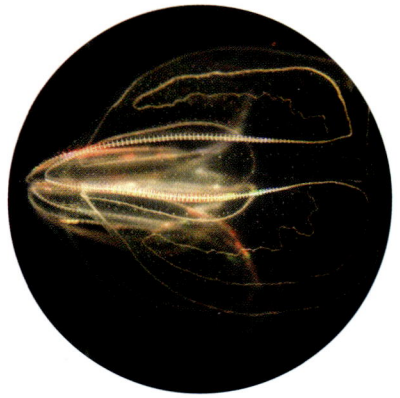

Illuminati
At right, female fireflies, also known as glowworms or lightning bugs, await suitors. Above, from top: the gills of jack o'lantern mushrooms emit green light in dark conditions; a Genji firefly signals to potential mates in Japan; a tiny comb jelly creates light to confuse predators.

reproduction

*The walnut-trunk, the walnut-husks, and the ripening or
 ripen'd long-round walnuts
The continence of vegetables, birds, animals,
The consequent meanness of me should I skulk or find myself indecent,
 while birds and animals never once skulk or find
 themselves indecent…*

—Walt Whitman, *Spontaneous Me*

On the verge *These fertilized eggs, or larvae, of an orange-fin anemonefish (Amphiprion chrysopterus) remain in the larval stage for only a day or two before they enter a juvenile phase*

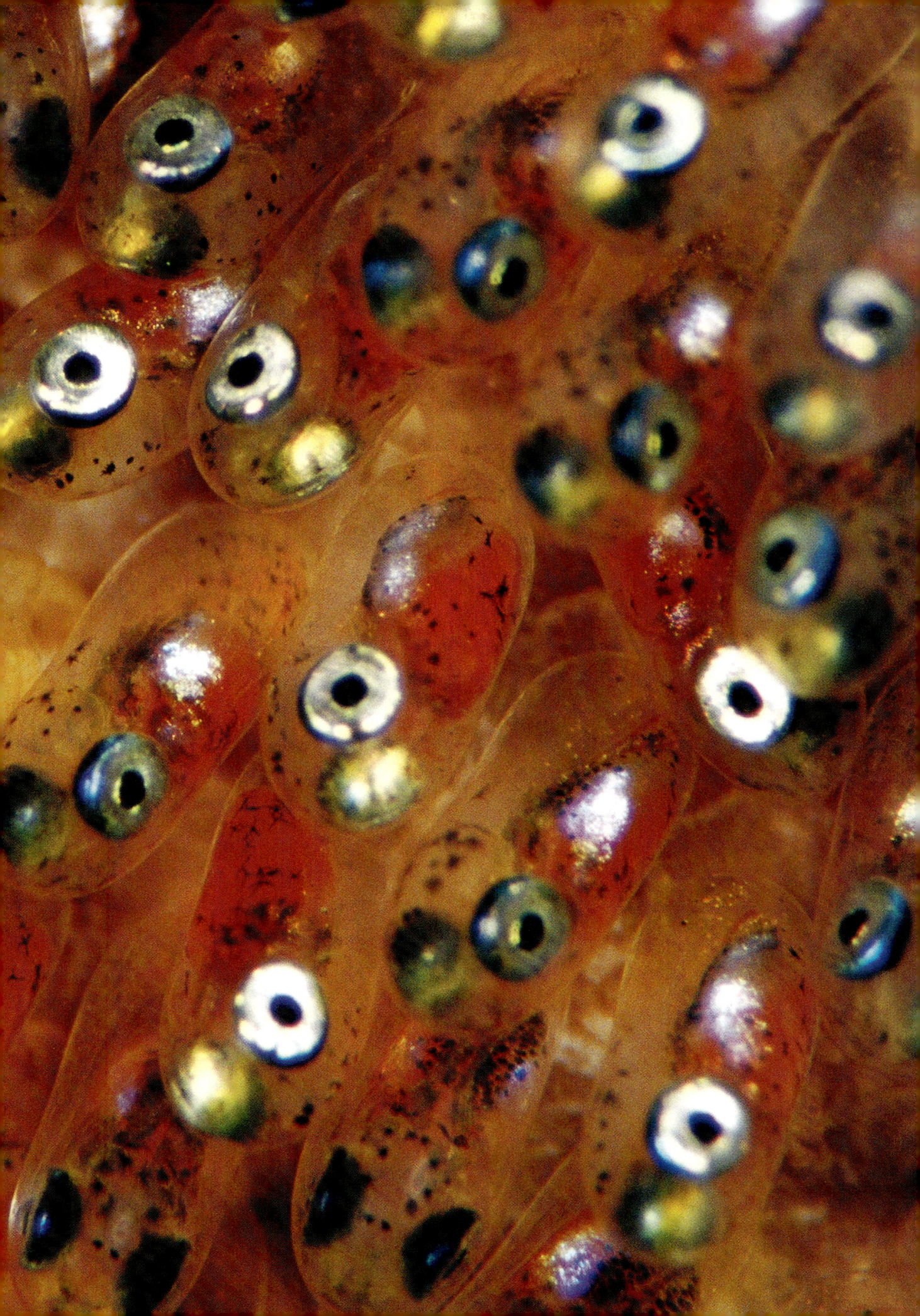

mating rites

Seals *Two male elephant seals square off—and sound off—in California*

Dustups for Dominance

Nature's great law of natural selection awards survival to the fittest specimens of a given species. We're used to thinking of natural selection as a process that occurs gradually over millions of years, as the offspring of better-adapted animals gradually outnumber those of the ill-adapted. But in fact, natural selection also takes place generation by generation among many species, as males engage in battles for dominance—and the right to mate with the most desirable females.

Generally speaking, male battles for dominance are seen among the more advanced animals, including many mammal species. In such groups, there is often one male that takes a leadership role: this alpha male is the only male in the group that is allowed to mate, and he will mate with every female in the group until he is ousted from his position by a stronger male.

In other cases, the alpha male bonds with an alpha female, and they are the primary mating pair. This is the case in most wolf packs, which are highly organized social units in which a variety of roles, most directly related to the activity of hunting in a pack, are clearly established. In some cases, several pairs in a pack of wolves may mate and breed, but more attention in the form of food, rearing and protection will be awarded to the offspring of the alpha pair. Male wolves that lose a battle for dominance often choose to leave the pack rather than assume an inferior position; these "lone wolves" then wander the countryside seeking a mate to help them begin a new pack structure. In some animals species, including apes, lone males band together in a social unit known as a bachelor group.

Male mating rituals are as diverse as the animal kingdom itself, and not all of them involve fighting. Some contests involve displays of grace, with males competing to show their prowess at leaping or running. But many more are duels in which the combatants resemble gladiators, wielding the weapons of their species: bull moose battle with antlers; seals with bellowing blasts from their vocal cords; rams with tough spiraling horns. Nature's challenge: Get ready to rumble, and may the best man win! ∎

Yahoo! *Two red-crowned cranes* (Grus japonensis) *raise their voices during a courtship dance in Hokkaido, Japan. The cranes are highly endangered; as few as 1,500 may survive in the wild*

courting rites

Bower power *A male bowerbird adds a dash of blue color to the elaborate structure he has built and decorated to woo a mate*

Desperately Seeking...

THINK OF IT AS ANIMAL ADVERTISING: JUST AS lonely humans place personal ads, wild creatures gripped by the urge to merge find countless ways to declare their availability and desirability. The poster boy for courting displays is the male peacock that struts and fans his colorful tail feathers when in search of a mate, but his behavior is far from unique. The chests of male gelada baboons turn a fiery shade of red during courtship. Frigatebirds inflate a large red bladder, the gular sac, beneath their chins, while some species of bellbird can stiffen three wattles that usually hang loosely from their heads, creating the appearance of tricorn spikes extending from the face, a sort of horizontal Mohawk. Several breeds of lizard not only puff up their throats like goiters but also raise their crests. Many birds, such as male ducks, molt and take on new, brighter plumage when mating season arrives.

But what of animals not born with the anatomical equipment to promote themselves? Male bowerbirds build complex structures from twigs, leaves and every other building material they can find, fill them with all the brightly colored objects they can scavenge, then present the bower to the female, who tours it before deciding whether to breed. Interestingly, the most ornate of these bridal chambers are built by the bowerbird species that has the dullest plumage and whose males are thus the least naturally equipped to draw the eye of a mate. Breeds with brighter feathers also build bowers, but they are far less intricate.

Charles Darwin once wrote, "The sight of a feather in a peacock's tail ... makes me sick," and little wonder: under his theory of natural selection, such lavish allocations of effort and biological resources can seem pointless. After all, a brighter coat or a talent for architecture doesn't help an animal find food or fight off competitors. This prompted Darwin to devise a second theory, which he called "sexual selection." It postulates that any trait that increases an individual's chance of mating is also reinforced, and thus is more likely to be passed on to subsequent generations. ∎

Great frigatebird *Inflating the red gular sac beneath his chin, this male* Fregata minor *seeks to attract the female next to him. These large birds are native to the tropics; their wingspan can reach 7.5 ft. (2.3 m). Once called man-of-war birds, frigatebirds received a nautical nomenclatural upgrade in the 19th century*

Hooded seal *This male seal is showing off his inflatable nasal membrane. The first word of its scientific name,* Cystophora cristata, *means "bladder bearer" in Greek. The hooded seal is found only in the Arctic and northern Canada*

Water lily reed frog Hyperolius pusillus *puffs up his resonant bladders in order to issue a loud mating call. In this case, the physical transformation is a courting rite based on sound rather than appearance*

Ring-necked pheasant *One would think his bright red face and the brilliant white ring around his neck might be enough to attract a mate, but this male* Phasianus colchicus *puts on quite a show of flapping his wings. Night fever!*

Safe and sound *Emperor penguins mate for life and share a complex parenting cycle. The mother lays a large egg, then leaves it in the father's care over the long Antarctic winter. The female returns when the chick hatches and watches over it alone, while the male departs. Later the father returns and both parents share in nurturing the chick*

 parenting

Family Ties

BIRDS DO IT. BEES DO IT. EVEN EDUCATED FLEAS do it. And after they've done it: well, there are a lot of little birds, bees and fleas to be raised. Parenting in nature assumes a wide variety of forms. Filmgoers around the world thrilled to the sacrificial ordeal endured by adult emperor penguins as they weathered the brutal Antarctic winter to protect their eggs in the hit 2006 documentary *March of the Penguins*. Yet for every heartwarming example of animals that mate for life and share in the nurturing of their young to independence, nature also seems to serve up a dystopian counterpart: animal parents that show little interest in their children and never create a meaningful bond with them.

In species in which fertilization takes place externally without sexual activity, as in many fish, there is little display of parenting behavior. In contrast, viviparous animals—those that give birth to live young—are likely to be deeply involved in the care and feeding of their offspring. However, the degree of parental involvement generally depends on the state of development of the newborn: mammals like giraffes and horses give birth to infants that are capable of standing and walking within an hour, whereas those that give birth to less fully developed children spend much more time caring for their young. Mammals, of course, are distinguished in the animal kingdom by the presence of female mammary glands and nutrition via nursing, which forges a strong link between parent and child.

Ovoviviparous animals, such as sharks and many reptiles, incubate their eggs within their bodies, then give birth to live young when the eggs hatch internally. Oviparous animals, including birds, lay fertilized eggs, then incubate them, generally with their body warmth, to begin development. Most birds carefully feed and nurture their young until they are independent enough to leave the nest; the tasks are so demanding that birds often enter into monogamous relationships, at least until the chicks are fledged, to see them through.

Lest we grow too misty-eyed over the extent to which animals can seem to mirror humans in their devotion to their young: biologists have observed infanticide, the killing of young by their parents, in many species. Oftentimes this takes the form of cannibalistic infanticide, in which parents kill and eat their offspring; the practice has been observed in chimpanzees, prarie dogs and pigs, to name only a few. To which we can only say, if feebly: Don't do it. ∎

Hummingbirds *Unlike most bird species, males are not involved in nesting*

Wolves *Born blind and deaf, pups remain in the den until about 2 months old*

Armadillos *Like humans, these armored critters are placental mammals, but their young grow up quickly, reaching maturity in three to six months*

Manatees *These aquatic mammals are pregnant for 12 months, and calves often are not fully weaned for 18 months. Above, a calf nurses*

marsupial parenting

Outback lookout
This young eastern gray kangaroo joey in Australia is almost old enough to leave the pouch

Womb With A View

MARSUPIAL BABIES ARE THE ULTImate pouch potatoes. Born very prematurely by human standards, the offspring of kangaroos, wombats and other marsupials have undeveloped hearts, lungs and kidneys that are not able to sustain life. These offspring are also stunningly small: some newborn kangaroos (a.k.a. joeys) are the size of bees, even though they will eventually be as tall as an adult human. The joey's only parts that are even close to maturity at birth are its chest muscles and forelimbs, which enable the tiny, blind child to crawl from the birth canal to a pouch (called a marsupium) on its mother's belly. Once inside, the baby affixes itself to a nipple, which expands to lock the newborn in place. Also sheltering and holding the child in position are muscles inside the pouch that form a kind of external womb.

This unusual nurturing strategy has many advantages for marsupials, which are adapted to harsh environments. If food becomes scarce, the mother stops producing milk and allows the baby to die. This doesn't hurt the mother's chances of reproduction, for many marsupial females keep several embryos on standby and will begin to develop another as soon as one dies. Infanticide also increases the mother's chances of survival: nature gives placental mammals like humans little choice other than to carry a baby to term, even if there's not enough food to support both mother and child.

A baby kangaroo usually pokes its head outside the mother's pouch around four months after it first crawled in. At five months, it takes its first, tentative steps on the ground, but it will continue living part time within the pouch (and nursing) until it is about a year old. After that, kangaroo moms will chase away a child that tries to climb back into the comforts of the pouch: it's time to grow up. ∎

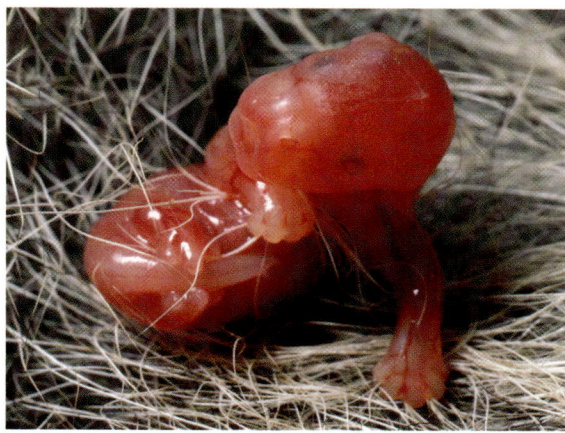

Newborn This tiny wallaby is about to take its most dangerous journey: across its mother's body to her pouch

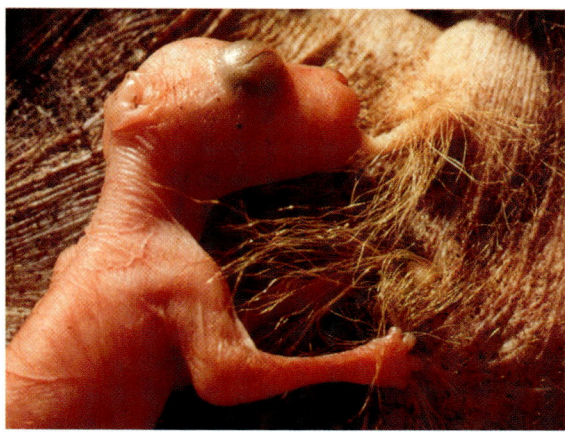

Attached A red kangaroo joey nurses within its mother's pouch

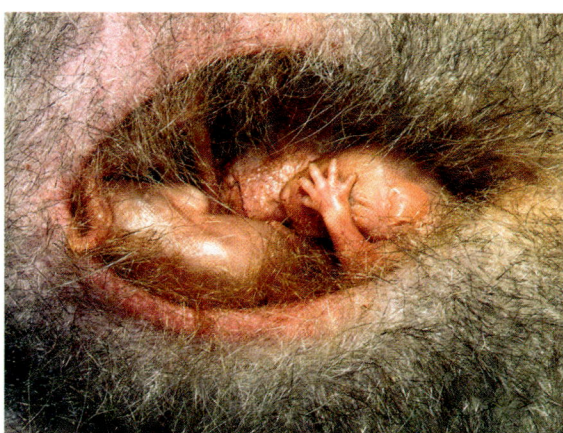

Resting A Virginia opossum sleeps in the pouch; opossums nurse for 3 months before leaving the pouch, kangaroos for much longer

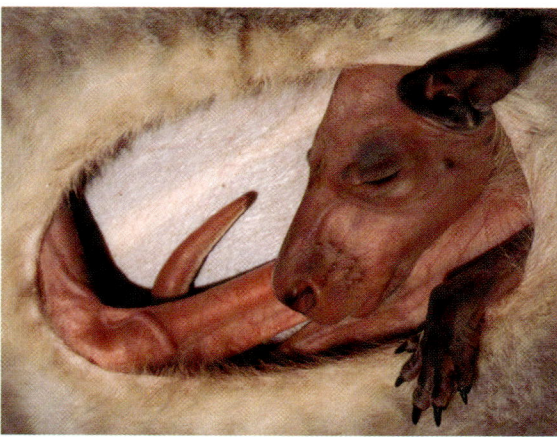

Snoozing A red kangaroo joey, about 130 days old, takes a nap in the pouch. At age 5 months or so, it will emerge for the first time

play

Never a Dull Moment

"HAPPINESS IS NEVER BETTER EXHIBITED," CHARLES Darwin wrote in *The Descent of Man*, "than by young animals, such as puppies, kittens, lambs, and company, when playing together, like our own children." The similarity is clear, yet animal behaviorists, or ethologists, still can't say why animals play.

Much play behavior in animals seems to be a dress rehearsal for adult needs like hunting, fighting for mates or escaping from predators. Such pantomime is seen most often in social species in which parents protect and feed their young. That includes most mammals and many species of birds. Yet even cockroaches have been observed chasing one another in a manner that some researchers believe might be play.

Most reptiles (with the exception of turtles) appear not to play at all. One theory posits that because they are cold-blooded and have lower metabolic rates, reptiles simply don't have any energy to spare. Indeed, the burn rate from play is considerable: some animals devote as much as 40% of their time and 3% of their total energy to horsing around. Call us unscientific, but perhaps they enjoy all that recess for the same reason that human kids do: It's fun, Mom! ∎

Where Seldom Is Heard a Discouraging Word

At top left, chimpanzee (Pan troglodytes) adults have been documented playing with their young in humanlike ways, making silly faces, tickling and making a sound that may be the primate equivalent of laughter. Below them are mother and child East African river hippos (Hippopotamus amphibious kiboko). These big mammals chase each other and spar in mock combat. They also, believe it or not, do underwater backflips.

On this page, the beluga whale (Delphinapterus leucas) at top is blowing a toroidal ring, which scientists believe is an act of pure play. At left, young vicuñas (Vicugna vicugna) in the Peruvian Andes simulate fighting like adult males vying for victuals. In the same manner, an America buffalo cow (Bison bison) squares off and butts heads with her calf, above.

fish reproduction

Jawfish Eggs
A male jawfish of genus Opistognathus *holds fertilized eggs in his mouth, protecting them from predators. Animals that incubate eggs in this fashion are classified as mouthbrooders; most such animals are fish, though some frogs also do so. It is often the male who takes on this duty. Jawfish live in burrows on the seabed that they excavate with their strong jaws.*

Swell Shark Baby
The egg case of this just-hatched blotchy swell shark (Cephaloscyllium umbratile) *is a flat rectangular shape. The baby shark is about 5 to 6 in. (13 to 15 cm) long; it has a double row of spiny denticles on its back to help break open the case. This newborn is blue, but it will take on a blotchy brown color as it matures. Swell sharks, like pufferfish, are named for their ability to inflate their bodies to deceive predators.*

Horn Shark Egg Case

The natural world abounds in lovely geometrical forms, such as this hard, spiral-shaped egg case of a horn shark (Heterodontus francisci). Such cases are screwed into crevices in undersea rocks; each holds a single shark, which will hatch in six to nine months. Horn sharks are slow-moving and a bit sluggish—for sharks, that is.

Seadragon Eggs

As is the case with a number of fish and amphibian species, the male common seadragon (Phyllopteryx taeniolatus) is charged with carrying the fertilized eggs. The female deposits the ruby-colored eggs on the ventral area of the male's tail, called a brood patch. When the eggs hatch, the young seadragons remain inside a yolk sac that nourishes them for several days.

metamorphosis

Ch-ch-ch-changes

NATURE IS A GRAND ILLUSIONIST, BUT THE PROCESS by which a creature's body is transformed into a radically different incarnation surpasses mere trickery: metamorphosis is more akin to a miracle. The change from tadpole to frog, or caterpillar to butterfly, not only requires that old limbs be discarded while new appendages sprout, but it also means that most of the original creature's internal organs and nervous system disappear, to be replaced by new equipment for moving, breathing, digesting food and carrying out many other essential tasks. More often than not, these tools are adapted to an entirely different environment and diet than were their predecessor's. The bad news: the transformation frequently makes the critter very tempting to an entirely new set of predators.

Metamorphosis is a stunning feat of genetic engineering. A butterfly's DNA contains the blueprint for both the the humble caterpillar of immaturity and the glorious winged adult it becomes. More remarkable, all these genes are switched on and off at precisely the right moment. The timing appears to be related to physical cues that the animal takes from its environment, especially light and temperature, which change in tandem with the seasons. Thus, as summer draws

Makeover *Monarch butterflies begin life as an egg, far left, that hatches into a caterpillar, which spins a silk cocoon, or chrysalis, third picture, in which it begins its transformation. The process concludes with the emergence of the adult winged insect*

near, a tadpole's tail begins to disappear, while legs start emerging and gills begin mutating into lungs. Its digestive tract is reconfigured to thrive on a carnivorous rather than vegetarian diet. Within weeks the fishlike creature is gone, replaced by an amphibian that hops instead of swims, breathes air instead of respires in water and eats insects rather than leaves.

Scientists have long wondered whether a creature's memories can survive the process of metamorphosis. In March 2008 that fascinating question was partially answered, in the affirmative, by findings published in the journal *PLoS ONE*. Researchers led by biologist Martha Weiss of Georgetown University trained tobacco hornworm caterpillars to fear the strong odor of nail-polish remover by exposing subjects to it while administering a mild electric shock. They found that caterpillars that received this conditioning early on did not transfer the memory after they were transformed into adult moths—but those that were shocked later in the caterpillar stage did retain the reflex and fled from the smell. The scientists hope these findings may help them learn how to reorganize human mental circuitry to better preserve our brain functions following an otherwise debilitating stroke. ■

seeds

They get around *At left, a coconut, or palm seed, takes root after floating ashore on Bora Bora. Below, from left: burrs catch a ride on a spaniel's ear; dandelion seeds are ready to go airborne; twin-bladed sycamore seeds, like maple seeds, are designed to rotate in midair*

Breeding by Seeding

PLANTS ARE SMARTER THAN PEOPLE, IT SEEMS, AT least in one respect: millions of years before humans invented the wheel, plants were utilizing most of the methods we later devised for getting around, and a few we've never quite mastered. The catch, of course, is that plants themselves don't move from place to place—their seeds do. And they accomplish this by rolling like wheels, riding on wind or water, being carried overland on the backs of animals and even by the plant equivalent of being shot from a cannon. They also fly in a way that human beings are unlikely ever to experience, by hitching rides with birds and insects.

Each autumn in the American West, tumbleweeds disconnect themselves from their roots (which survive to flower again the following spring) and somersault vast distances across the plains, spreading seeds for a new generation of the species. Other seeds, like those of the maple tree, take to the air. Their leaf is the shape of a helicopter blade, causing the seed not to fall directly to the ground, where it might fail to take root, but to rotate a good distance away from the parent tree. Other aviation models include the glider: the two-winged seed of the Asian climbing gourd *Alsomitra macrocarpa* flies in circles around the rain forest. The parachute is also popular: numerous plant species, such as the dandelion, sprout seeds with light, umbrella-shaped crowns of filament that can keep them airborne for miles.

Some seeds find a place to take root by methods nautical rather than aeronautical. Mangrove trees drop their seeds into the flowing waters of their swampy homes, the better to be carried downstream. And coconuts have been documented to travel thousands of miles across open ocean before taking root on distant tropical islands, like the plant at left.

Some plants use animals as their beasts of burden: the adhesive fabric Velcro was famously inspired when a Swiss engineer returned from a hunting trip determined to find out why the seeds of the burdock plant kept sticking to his clothes and his dog's hair. He found that the burrs were covered with microscopic hooks designed to cling to animal fur and thus be transported to distant locations to root. And some plants literally go ballistic: several species of orchid allow their seedpods to shrivel until their skins crack from the tension. The resulting burst can hurl seeds more than 50 ft. (15 m) away. ■

 pollination

Where the Bee Sucks …
The honeybee above is in heaven—bee heaven, that is—as it gathers nectar from a pumpkin blossom. The sweet nectar and bright color are the lures that attract the bee into the flower, where it brushes up against pollen, finely grained powder that sticks to the insect and contains male gametes. Later the bee may rub against the carpel of this or another flower, which holds the female reproductive organs, thus transferring the pollen and beginning the process of fertilization. The bee plays the role of middleman and is called a pollinator. Pollination is critical to agriculture around the world—which is why the ongoing decline of the bee population in the U.S. caused by a syndrome called colony collapse disorder is of grave concern not only to botanists and beekeepers but to the nation's farmers as well.

The Bill and the Blossom

The long bill of the green-breasted mango (Anthracothorax prevostii), a type of hummingbird, perfectly fits into the long horizontal blossoms of a heliconia flower in the Costa Rican rain forest. The birds, bees and other animals that help flowers reproduce by spreading their pollen are called biotic pollinators. When pollination occurs without the aid of a living intermediary—for instance, when pollen is spread by the wind—it is called abiotic pollination. Designed for their labors as biotic pollinators, hummingbirds are unique among the bird kingdom: they beat their wings in a figure-eight pattern, which allows them not only to hover in mid-air as they collect nectar but also to fly backward and upside down.

fungi

In a Class of Their Own

HUMAN BEINGS LIKE TO THINK OF THEMSELVES as the dominant life-form on the planet, but fungi—the kingdom that includes mushrooms, yeasts, molds and lichen—may be gaining on us. Tightly woven into our daily lives, they're in the beer and wine we drink and the bread and cheese we eat; they're in the drugs we take, from antibiotics to statins; they're in the fuel, pesticides and preservatives we manufacture. Nor are we alone: thousands of species of plants and animals depend on fungi in ways that scientists are only beginning to understand. What they have not begun to understand is the startling chemical properties of many species of fungi. Some of them, for instance, can ingest granite, tar, fog or uranium and transform them back into basic elements or lock them into a stable, harmless form.

Indeed, fungi are now regarded as a major form of life on Planet Earth. In recent decades, taxonomists revised the definition that divided the "tree of life" into animal and vegetable kingdoms and created a third branch for fungi, which for centuries had been regarded as plants. The change was driven by a surprising discovery that emerged from DNA analysis in the 1990s: fungi have more in common genetically

Toxic Toadstools

The colorful fly agaric (Amanita muscaria) *at left is a hallucinogen—Rasputin was a fan. It is sufficiently toxic that it was once used as an insecticide, sprinkled in milk to attract flies. Mushrooms are a staple in cuisines around the world, and while there are many toxic species of mushrooms, only a few are strong enough to be deadly to humans.*

Many species of mushrooms are "puffballs," explosively exhaling millions of microscopic spores at a time, like the earthstar mushroom (Geastrum triplex), *above in Spain. Fungi reproduce in a variety of ways, both sexual and asexual, and some fungi adopt their mode of reproduction to local conditions.*

with animals, including humans, than with plants.

Fungi are pervasive on the planet. While hundreds of thousands of species of have been identified, scientists estimate that perhaps 1 million more are yet to be identified. They surround us (and sometimes inhabit us), almost always unseen. Estimated to constitute fully one-quarter of the total biomass of dense forests, microscopic fungal spores coat every surface of the ecosystem. If the trees and soil were somehow to be removed while they remained, an observer would still be able to see a ghostly forest, outlined by spores.

The most familiar fungi are mushrooms, which are the visible reproductive organs of a more extensive organism, the mycelium, an invisibly fine web of long, threadlike structures, or hyphae, buried within a host medium, such as a log or soil. In most cases, each of these mushroom "fruiting bodies" contains millions of spores, both male and female. When they are released into the wind, spores that land on a suitable host begin to germinate, forming hyphae, which begin burrowing into the host. Yet that's not enough to form a mycelium that can reproduce itself: only when a male spore and a female spore meet and combine is there hope for a new subject in the kingdom of 'shrooms. ∎

feeding

The world below the brine;
Forests at the bottom of the sea—the branches and leaves,
Sea-lettuce, vast lichens, strange flowers and seeds—the thick
    tangle, the openings, and the pink turf,
Different colors, pale gray and green, purple, white, and gold—
    the play of light through the water
                —Walt Whitman, *The World Below the Brine*

Snack time *A sea anemone (Urticinopsis antarctica) feeds by moving food to its mouth with its tentacles. Anemones are cnidarians, related to jellyfish and corals*

raptors

Gotcha! *A bald eagle snatches a fish from the waters off the Kenai Peninsula in Alaska, displaying all the natural advantages that make raptors the apex predators in many ecosystems: strong, large talons to grip; eyesight so powerful the bird can see fish under the surface of the sea; a wingspan of more than 8 ft. (2.5 m), allowing the speedy bird to strike without warning. Another attribute, the eagle's strong bill, helps it tear into its victims' bodies. Hawks and owls, vultures and buzzards are also raptors, though some of these fierce carnivores, like buzzards, primarily feed on carrion*

hunting strategies

Killer whale, sea lion

Python, gazelle

Bobcat, muskrat

Predator and Prey

NATURE'S BOUNDLESS CREATIVITY IS DISPLAYED memorably in the adaptations and behaviors that allow animals to dwell in a wide variety of very different environments. And it's also on view when many of them pursue a task that is essential to their survival: hunting for food. In their strategies of pursuit and capture, animals deploy a fascinating arsenal of weapons, ruses, tactics and abilities.

Consider snakes, whose lack of appendages might seem to inhibit hunting. That's not a problem for the python above: after dropping from a tree limb onto an adult gazelle, it exerts a power of constriction strong enough to strangle its prey. The python's jaws open so wide it can then engulf the constricted gazelle. Or look at the archerfish, whose name reveals his unique tactic: from beneath the surface of a pond, he sprays an insect from a leafy perch into his watery element (and mouth).

Many animals hunt in groups; wolf packs are highly efficient organizations for stalking and killing prey, with specific roles—and equivalent shares of the kill—assigned to each member. Killer whales hunt both in pods and as individuals; the orca shown above is a lone ranger chasing a sea lion. In some animals the hunting instinct is so strong that they toy with their victims. Felines, ranging in size from a bobcat tormenting a wounded muskrat to a house cat pawing with a cornered mouse, are among nature's most remorseless killers: they insist on playing with their food. ■

Archerfish, insect

predators

Last gasp *Outmatched, outraced and outweighed, this kudu, a type of antelope, is also out of time: it will soon succumb to the lioness that is attacking it on the Serengeti plain in Africa*

spiderwebs

Fatal geometry *The majority of spiderwebs, like this one, are oval-shaped. Scientists have tried for decades to replicate spider silk; success could have uses ranging from surgical sutures to body armor*

Tough stuff *Tiger spiders reinforce their webs with heavy silk, or stabilimentum, to add strength, attract prey and frighten predators*

My parlor *Spiders that build funnel-shaped webs are most common in Asia and Australia. Their strong venom can harm humans*

Bubble *Water spiders spin a silk diving bell that holds enough air for its builder to breathe underwater for extended periods*

Snared *Net-casting spiders of the family Deinopidae build webs they suspend between their front legs, then toss to entangle a victim*

Worldwide Webs

SPIDERWEBS ARE AMONG NATURE'S NIFTIEST hunting tools, but they are far more than simple traps for catching dinner. For spiders, many of whom are blind, these sensory nets provide information, aid communication, offer transportation, help advertise for mates, serve as nurseries for young and in some cases provide underwater breathing chambers. In short, they are natural wonders that scientists are, in many ways, only beginning to understand.

There are some 40,000 known species of spiders, and many more may yet be discovered. Fewer than half of them build webs, but all spin silk, and most of them produce several specialized varieties. Spider silk is stronger than steel cable of equal width, more flexible than rubber and more stretchable than nylon. Some spiders spin 1,000 ft. (300 m) or more of silk each day.

The most familiar kind of web is made by "orb builders," which start with radial beams that resemble spokes on a wheel and support the structure, then dress them with spiral threads that funnel inward. These are coated with a strong glue that snags and holds insect prey. Most webs are so insubstantial that they must be rebuilt from scratch each day, so many of these eight-legged arachnids recycle: they eat the old web, then use its raw material to help recharge their silk glands and build a new one. ■

carnivorous plants

Vegans: Not!

THE MOTH IN THE PICTURE AT LEFT IS SECONDS AWAY FROM A fateful surprise. Attracted by the sweet-smelling nectar of the pitcher plant, the creature will fly into the aromatic orifice of the plant, only to discover that the aperture is a mouth, and it is now prey. The sides of the cavern into which it has fallen are slippery; at its bottom is a small body of liquid that first drowns, then dissolves, the moth. In some cases, pitcher plants contain insect larvae that help digest the prey.

There is a creepy quality to carnivorous plants: it's a rare 12-year-old boy who isn't fascinated by the allure of the Venus's flytrap, the most widely known of the insect-trapping plants. Perhaps it's the sense that these plants' clever hunting tactics—the inviting aroma, the false visual stimuli that telegraph "nectar" to hungry insects, the cleverly wrought trapping mechanism—seem the result of conscious artifice on the plants' part rather than adaptations resulting from natural selection. But of course it's the latter: the distinguishing quality of all carnivorous plants is that they are found in areas where the soil is not rich in nutrients, and thus the plants have been adapted to seek nutrition from alternate sources, such as insects.

Carnivorous plants feature a variety of trapping mechanisms. Some boast leaves that act much like flypaper to which their prey adheres. The Venus's flytrap has special hinged leaves, called snap traps, that close upon their victim once special trigger hairs are activated. Bladderworts have suction traps with hinged doors that open only one way—the way to death. ∎

Going, going ... *Botanists have identified nine distinct families and some 600 species of carnivorous plants. At top, a damselfly is trapped on the sticky tentacles of a spoonleaf sundew plant* (Drosera intermedia), *an example of a flypaper-style trap. The tentacles can bend to aid in enfolding the prey.*

Above, the hinges of a Venus's flytrap (Dionaea muscipula) *close upon a victim. The trigger hairs that spring the trap are very sensitive; two hairs must be touched in quick succession before the lobes snap shut*

defensive strategies

Go Ahead, Make My Day

Nature's challenge to most animals is harsh: eat or be eaten. Yet that stern necessity has fostered the development of a host of fascinating strategies animals rely on to avoid becoming prey. Some resort to camouflage, blending in with their surroundings to avoid detection; some mimic deadly plants or animals; others, like the pufferfish, are themselves poisonous. Some, like Africa's wildebeests, herd together to increase the odds of survival for each, or, like Alaska's musk oxen when stalked, form an outward-facing circle to protect the young within. Some, like skunks, release noxious odors. A few, like opossums, play dead. Others, like armadillos, shellfish and turtles, wear armor. Some, like octopuses, rely on stealth, releasing a smoke screen of ink to cloak their getaway. And some, like many species of antelope, rely on sheer speed to outrun predators.

In scientific terms, primary defensive equipment is always in place, like a porcupine's quills, while secondary defenses are behaviors switched on only when the animal feels danger is near, as when a hedgehog rolls into a ball to protect its softer organs. ∎

Quills and Chills

Top left, the porcupine's spiky, defensive quills are echoed by the stickers on a Diodon holocanthus, *above, whose common name is long-spine porcupinefish. The quills of North American porcupines can be 3 in. (8 cm) long; those of the Cape porcupine (*Hystrix africaeaustralis*), above, are even longer.*

At right, a Pacific giant octopus (Enteroctopus dofleini) *sprays a cloud of ink that will not only help mask its movements but will also dull a predator's sense of smell. At left, striped skunks (*Mephitis mephitis*) spray a foul-smelling liquid from their anal scent glands that can blind predators.*

camouflage

Boreal Owl

Scarlet Windowed Moth

Green Vine Snake

Spiny Bug

Giant Anteater

Now You See Them...

NOW YOU DON'T: NOWHERE IS THE POWER OF natural selection displayed more memorably than in the elaborate use of camouflage by animals. The proposition is easy enough to understand: a creature that blends into its natural habitat has a much better chance of catching its prey, or of avoiding its predators, if it can't be seen. What surprises us is the extent of the diversity and detail that go into creating these visual ruses. The scarlet windowed moth not only matches the color of the autumn leaves in its native forest habitats but also matches the striations of the individual leaves.

The two varieties of katydids featured here couldn't look less related: the bottle-green insect that dwells in the tropical jungle has the smooth look of a banana leaf. But the lichen-mimic katydid is rough and scaly, like the lichen in its wet habitat high in Ecuador's Andes; its wings closely resemble a twig. Like polar bears and arctic wolves, arctic hares take on the white hue of their snowy habitat in winter. Nature's costume party operates in animals large and small: like the tiny katydid, a 6-ft. (1.8 m)-long giant anteater lumbering through the South American pampas has been shaped over the centuries to blend into its native habitat. ■

Arctic Hares

Giant Walking Stick

Lichen-Mimic Katydid

Katydid

Hiding in Plain Sight

Boreal Owl
Aegolius funereus, also known as Tengmalm's owl, is a smallish owl that lives in coniferous forests, blending into the bark of the trees it calls home.

Anteater
At 6 ft. (1.8 m) in length, *Myrmecophaga tridactyla* is the largest of the four types of anteaters, creatures whose order, Pilosa, includes sloths.

Green Vine Snake
Oxybelis fulgidus dwells in South American rain forests.

Spiny Bug
Pephricus livingstone shares the spiky-yet-silky look of the delicate pink grasses of its forested habitat.

Scarlet Windowed Moth
Cricula andrei mimics the color and shape of tree leaves.

Arctic Hare
The white winter coat of *Lepus arcticus* matches the polar landscape; its summer coat is a mottled brown.

Giant Walking Stick
Megaphasma dentricus is at home in tall prairie grass.

Katydid
This member of the vast Tettigoniidae family has both the color and striations of the banana leaf it is walking on.

Lichen-Mimic Katydid
Its rough skin resembles the lichen of the Ecuadorean forest.

camouflage

Leafy Sea Dragon

Harlequin Crab

Pygmy Seahorse

Marine Masquerades

WHILE IT'S COMMONPLACE FOR HUMAN BEINGS to project their behavior onto animals, it's a mistake to employ anthropomorphism too broadly in approaching the animal kingdom. It's tempting to assume that the marine creatures shown here have chosen to disguise themselves in order to hunt better—or, in most cases, better evade their hunters. But alligators don't decide what skin color is in vogue this season: that hue has been decided over vast timespans by the process of natural selection, which favors animals whose outward appearance makes them more apt to survive.

The results can be breathtaking, as fish indigenous to coral reefs come to resemble the reefs themselves, and the American alligator's tough hide bears the same greenish tint as the marshy ponds of the Everglades it swims in. The leafy sea dragon, at top left, is one of nature's most fascinating eye-foolers: it sports a number of extra appendages that look like leaves but serve no function other than to make the creature blend in amid the seaweed of its natural habitat. In some cases the adaptations are extreme: the eyes and mouth of the stargazer are located on top of its head, so that this bottom-feeder lies prone in the seabed. ■

Sand Stargazer

Painted Frogfish

American Alligator

Adaptation: Concealment

Leafy Sea Dragon
Phycodurus eques mimics the look of native seaweed in Australian waters to fool predators. Related to the seahorse, the sea dragon can grow to 18 in. (45 cm) in size.

Harlequin Crab
The brown spots and ivory background of *Lissocarcinus orbicularis* ape the coloration of the sea cucumber it is crawling upon in the picture above left, taken off Borneo.

Pygmy Seahorse
Hippocampus bargibanti blends in perfectly with the red tubercles of the pink coral host it feeds upon, gorgonian coral found off Australia. It is indeed a pygmy form, topping off at less than 1 in. (2.5 cm) in size.

Sand Stargazer
This member of the family Dactyloscopidae looks scary, but it's a small animal, at under 4 in. (10 cm) in length.

Painted Anglerfish (Frogfish)
The bright orange *Antennarius pictus* resembles the sponges among which it lives. In the picture above, the fish's head is on the left, and its tail is on the right.

American Alligator
The nubby skin of *Alligator mississippiensis* blends in with the duckweed that coats this pond in the Everglades. Unlike many of the camouflaged critters shown here, the alligator is very large: a full-grown adult can be 14.5 ft. (4.4 m) long and weigh as much as 750 lbs. (340 kg).

color-changing animals

Veiled Chameleon
This large species of the lizard family is perhaps the best known of those animals whose skins change color. But like the veiled chameleon (Chamaeleo calyptratus) at left, these lizards do not change their "spots" at will to disguise themselves by blending in with their surroundings. Instead, scientists say, the color change expresses their physiological state and perhaps is used to attract mates and to communicate.

Mimic Octopus
Most species of octopus are highly flexible, but Thaumoctopus mimicus is one of nature's greatest shape-shifters: it is able to assume the form and coloration of at least 15 other species, including crabs, stingrays and jellyfish. Its powers of mimicry are so strong it was not recognized as a distinct species until the late 1990s; before that, duped scientists mistook it for the animals it was imitating.

Giant Cuttlefish
Sepia apama is one of the sea's oddities; a cephalopod (like octopuses and squid), it has eight long prehensile arms that sprout from its head, highly developed eyes and a unique internal shell, the cuttlebone. These so-called chameleons of the sea can change the color of their skin with blinding rapidity, an ability they use to communicate and to camouflage themselves from predators.

Canopy *Raindrops keep falling on its head, so this red-eyed tree frog (Agalychnis callidryas), takes cover under a leaf in the rain forest and gives it a hand in holding the elements at bay*